COOKING UNDER FIRE

The following recipes appear courtesy of their original publishers:

"Bibb Lettuce with a Shower of Roquefort Cheese" from *The Olives Table* by Todd English and Sally Sampson. New York: Simon & Schuster, 1997.

"*Blue Ginger* Crispy Calamari," from *Simply Ming: Easy Techniques for East-Meets-West Meals* by Ming Tsai and Arthur Boehm. New York: Clarkson Potter, 2003.

"Pâté de Campagne" from *Charcuterie: The Craft of Salting, Smoking, and Curing* by Michael Ruhlman and Brian Polcyn. New York: W.W. Norton, 2005.

Library of Congress Cataloging-in-Publication Data is available upon request.

WGBH Educational Foundation
125 Western Avenue
Boston, MA 02134

Visit our web site at www.wgbh.org

ISBN: 1-59375-391-8

First Edition

10   9   8   7   6   5   4   3   2

Printed in the United States of America

The recipes included in this book have not been tested by WGBH.

Recipes and Behind-the-Scenes
At PBS's Sizzling New Reality Series

WGBH Educational Foundation
Boston, Massachusetts

Contents

Cooking Under Fire: Recipes and Behind-the-Scenes at PBS's Sizzling New Reality Series

Recipes from the Finalists

The finalists crowd the kitchen preparing their dishes.

The finalists line up for evaluation by the judges.

Introduction:
A Word from the Executive Producers

Chefs have achieved a kind of rock-and-roll status in the last decade. No longer are they simply the anonymous culinary hands behind the kitchen door. Restaurant chefs have stepped up front-and-center and claimed a new kind of celebrity. Television has played a decisive role in making this kind of fame possible. Granted, it didn't happen overnight. It began with none other than the beloved French Chef, Julia Child, who flipped her first omelet before a television audience in 1963. Julia's pioneering public television series, *The French Chef*, became a staple on the television dial, and gave rise to what would eventually become an entire cable food industry.

What was it that catapulted Julia, arguably America's first real celebrity chef, and a long list of other television luminaries, to culinary fame? Was it their undeniable charm and ability to connect with the viewer? Or was it their finely honed culinary skills, combined with a contagious love of food that communicated itself across the airwaves? We believe that the celebrity chefs who have achieved stardom—both on and off TV—have all these skills and more. To survive the heat of the kitchen, you need a unique and creative style, tremendous business acumen, a strong vision, the leadership ability to guide others in the direction you want to go, and unadulterated passion combined with the endurance to get the job done day in and day out.

Celebrity Chefs: The Times They Are A-Changing

Making it and then surviving as a world-class chef is a tough row to hoe. That reality often gets obscured by the glitz and glamour, and as a result aspiring chefs often underestimate the difficulty of the path to success.

In order to excel as a chef, says Todd English, "your work ethic becomes as important as your talent." Ming Tsai adds that you also need "passion, patience, and a whole lot of ambition, combined with confidence and an indispensable sense of humor." Todd adds that "it's amazing how so many great chefs go out of business because they forgot to think about the mighty bottom line."

Cooking Under Fire was born out of a desire to enlighten viewers about the realities of being a chef in the fast-paced, demanding restaurant business. The industry is now the nation's largest private-sector employer (12.2 million employees). Fully two out of five American adults have worked in a restaurant at some point in their lives. Even so, most of us have only a partial understanding of the role of a chef, especially in a successful restaurant. We decided to focus on the making of a world-class chef—and to provide a clearer understanding of why only the deserving few ultimately survive.

Finalist Matthew Leeper shows his mise en place to the judges.

A Show Is Born

Served up by National Public Television as "reality television that feeds the brain," this documentary-style series was designed as TV for food lovers, and for those who want to discover a

side of the restaurant business they have never seen. It was also created as unscripted television that would reveal the intense pressure and complex skills needed to succeed as a chef in the country's top kitchens.

How did the series play itself out? Each week for twelve weeks, a panel of celebrity chefs presented the twelve finalists a varied and intense series of cooking challenges—from "cooking on the line" to preparing "the meal of your lifetime" to demonstrating a fundamental ability to listen and follow directions. Endurance also played a part: to survive and excel, our finalists were asked to execute demanding culinary tasks while traveling across the country, working long hours with little sleep. What evolved was a non-stop coast-to-coast competition that took our judges and finalists from fish markets and fruit stands to a variety of restaurant kitchens in the nation's culinary capitals: Los Angeles, Las Vegas, Miami, and New York.

The challenges were made even more difficult by adding some rigorous constraints: a ticking clock, a limited budget, or an exceedingly cramped physical space.

Of course, we made sure there was a bright light at the end of the tunnel. Success at each challenge would bring the remaining contenders one step closer to the coveted prize: a chef position at one of Todd English's New York City restaurants. Failure entailed a risk of being "86ed"—in restaurant parlance, sent home.

The competition proved both grueling and exciting. We went with the conceit that you can't have a reality show—even one that pushes the envelope—without sabotage, anger, and even seeing things go up in flames.

The Co-Hosts/Judges

In every episode, the finalists appeared before a panel of three judges.

Leading the panel was **Ming Tsai**, an Emmy-award-winning chef and host of the National Public Television series SIMPLY MING. Ming's passion for food was forged while working at the family restaurant in Dayton, Ohio. He went on to earn a degree in mechanical engineering at Yale, but never strayed far from cooking. That passion led him to study at Le Cordon Bleu cooking school in Paris, and ultimately to open the critically acclaimed restaurant Blue Ginger with his wife Polly.

Joining forces with Ming was **Todd English**, who owns or co-owns more than seventeen restaurants worldwide. Todd started cooking at fifteen and attended the Culinary Institute of America. After working and traveling in Italy, Todd developed a unique style of Mediterranean cooking that draws on his Italian heritage. Todd has won James Beard Awards as a Rising Star Chef and

the Best Chef of the Northeast, as well as critical acclaim for his restaurants. As the winner's future employer, Todd had a vested interest in the finalists' performance!

The third co-host/judge, **Michael Ruhlman**, came to the world of cooking from the perspective of a writer with an enormous appreciation for food. A self-proclaimed "amateur chef since fourth grade," Michael wrote *The Making of a Chef*, about how the oldest and most influential professional cooking school in the country, the Culinary Institute of America (CIA), trains its chefs. His research entailed going through the rigors of the program himself. For his *Soul of a Chef*, Michael researched the lives of professional working chefs.

COOKING UNDER FIRE

Judges Michael, Ming, and Todd enjoy what they're seeing.

The Guest Judges

In addition to the three co-hosts/judges, local chefs in each of the competition cities were asked to present to and work with the finalists and then to weigh in on the deliberations. Among them were chefs **David Myers** of Sona in Los Angeles, **Govand Armstrong** of Table 8 in Los Angeles, **Michael Mina** of Mina's in Las Vegas and San Francisco, **Michelle Bernstein** of Azul in Miami, **Frank Randazzo** of South Florida's Tallulah, and **Norman Van Aken** of Norman's in Miami, Orlando, and Los Angeles.

Collectively, these judges brought to the table the knowledge, understanding, talent, and skills necessary to instruct the finalists. They had also "walked the walk," having lived through the process of starting out and ultimately thriving in the restaurant business. As such, they recognize the skill and the passion it takes to make it as a world-class chef.

The Finalists

Anyone with natural talent or the drive to operate his or her own restaurant could apply to be on the show. But because we were looking for the next great American chef, we knew our finalist would need to have considerable experience. They would also need a demonstrated ability to handle the pressure that stepping into a high-drive New York City restaurant would demand.

To find the best prospects for our competition, we launched a nationwide search. Teams of casting agents were given the mission of finding a rising culinary superstar. And who would it ultimately be? We all speculated: A stay-at-home mom whose gastronomic skills were yet to be recognized? A culinary student with talent and vision but desperately in need of just this kind of opportunity?

After culling hundreds of candidates, our best prospects included culinary-school grads, seasoned restaurant talent, and even a nice cross-section of everyday foodies. These contenders went on to the next step—an audition before our panel of judges. We started out slow, asking each finalist to bring in a favorite ingredient or dish, or to talk about a prized cooking tool.

Applicants were also asked to describe their "passion for food," and to tell us why they viewed themselves as "the next rising star." Some candidates shied away; others stepped up without hesitation. Amy was among those who bravely stated her case: "What makes me think I can be (the next) great American chef? I can get a squad of six hard-headed men to do what I need them to do: 'You chop this.' 'You cook the rice.' 'No, don't put that in there.' Granted, some of my southern charm helps ease people's minds. I know you're supposed to be harsh in New York, but maybe I could smile them to death. When in doubt, use sugar."

COOKING
UNDER FIRE

The judges then tested the prospective finalists on their basic culinary skills: Can you identify, by smell, these twenty spices that are frequently used in American cuisine? Can you handle a knife skillfully? Show us by breaking down a salmon—one stroke, no nooks or crannies. How about taking this onion and doing a tidy little quarter-inch dice? Even these, the most fundamental of skills, yielded some surprising results. One reluctant candidate looked the salmon right in the eye and said, "I'm afraid I'm going to butcher this thing." (And butcher it she did.) Another contender provided her own blow-by-blow commentary: "I may be pretty, but I guess I sure can't dice."

The applicants were also thrown a few curve balls—just to see how well they could handle the pressure. We asked them to identify several obscure ingredients, including the sea cucumber. Very few could identify the thing, but the ways they problem-solved provided insight into them as people and as food detectives. When stumped, some reacted with anger; others approached it like a scientist. Some gave up at the start ("I have never seen such a thing.") While others proffered answers that were all over the map—from sea slug to cocoa bean to petrified tongue.

The quality of the finalists we ultimately selected was far richer than we could have imagined. People from every walk of life, and with all levels of experience. Even the most inexperienced among them had the guts and determination to try to make the leap to the top. We hadn't anticipated finding candidates of such quality and integrity.

Some finalists were true culinary artists, and saw themselves as such. "The plate is my canvas," finalist Blair King said, "and the tongs my paints and paintbrush, so to speak." He added, "While cooking, I get to use all five of my senses. I get to put the oil in the pan, and when the smoke comes up, I can see right then—bam, I'm using my sight. I throw the garlic in, bam. I hear if the plate's hot or not. I put meat in, sear the meat, and I can feel when it's medium-rare."

Other candidates were playful, even a bit cocky. John Paul Abernathy, the self-proclaimed "best damn line cook in Seattle," is a prime example. He was not afraid to admit that "cooking for the ladies became my forte" and that "a huge success to my early love life came from being able to wow women with food." But even John Paul knew that it takes more than attitude to climb to the top in a restaurant kitchen. Inspired by the vineyards and culinary influences of his native Napa Valley, John Paul's passion for cooking led him to cooking stints in France and Switzerland and ultimately to the Culinary Institute of America.

Confidence and leadership abilities also seemed abundant in many of our finalists, including French-born finalist Yannick Marchand. Yannick had grown up in the nurturing environment of his grandmother's kitchen. A graduate of the New England Culinary Institute, Yannick had been an avid cook ever since arriving in America more than fifteen years ago. Although he had years of professional cooking under his belt, he was eager for a new challenge. After sizing up the competition, he homed in on a well-cultivated strategy: "Don't forget it's good to have a beginner's mind," he said at the opening ceremony. "Always be a beginner and whatever you feel like, it's a new experience."

Katsuji Tanabe balked at the idea of being perceived as a beginner. "I've already proved to myself that I am good," he told our producers early on. "And now I (just) need to prove to someone else that I am good." That someone else probably includes his father. Katsuji, the son of a mechanical engineer, had bucked the expectation that he follow in his father's footsteps. Katsuji's love of food drove him to start out, in his words, "from the bottom up," by volunteering as a dishwasher in a professional kitchen. With a lot on the line, Katsuji urgently wanted to win the competition

Airborne Ranger Matthew Leeper grew up on Clark Air Force Base in the Philippines. During his stint in the Army, his love of cooking gave him a new direction at a difficult time. A committed Ranger, Matthew had developed severe joint pain on heavy road marches and night duty. But pride, he said, wouldn't allow him to reconsider his commitment to his fellow officers. A new path

COOKING UNDER FIRE

Judges and finalists gather on the first day of the competition.

opened up when Matthew was given the opportunity to work at the Ranger dining facility. The job was demanding—10–16 hours a day for nearly three years—but it was there that he met his mentor, a sergeant who was competing for a culinary Olympic gold. That man inspired Matthew to go to culinary school.

Though the world of the professional chef is distinctly male-dominated—only one in ten jobs is held by a woman—a sizeable turnout of female applicants proved anxious to cast their toques in the ring. Katie Hagen Whelchel, a self-described "classy redneck" who had grown up in Kentucky and spent five years working her way up through the kitchens of New York, hoped that into-the-frying-pan experience would give her an edge.

Native Californian Sara Lawson describes herself as someone always on the lookout for her next meal. Having decided that her purpose in life is "to learn, teach, laugh, and eat," Sara is driven by the desire to open her own restaurant someday. And then there was Autumn Maddox. Born in the small town (300-plus residents) of Custer, Washington, Autumn grew up surrounded by food. Her family grew corn, onions, chilies, strawberries and her personal favorite, green peas, on ten acres of land. Less to her liking was the fact that some of the cattle they raised ended up on their plates. "I remember one year we had a little baby cow, and I watched him grow. My dad called him Rib-Steak."

Our finalists had distinctly different backgrounds and skill levels, but certain qualities stood out as "universals" among them: they were all passionate about food, and they all had an unwavering determination to win.

The Challenges

After the auditions, each of *Cooking Under Fire*'s 11 subsequent half-hour shows was structured around a specific culinary challenge. The finalists had no idea what the challenges would be—but they did know they would face twelve intense days of cooking that would call on all of their experience, energy, and creativity. By joining the competition, they were submitting to a form of "culinary boot camp" very much akin to what they would face working as a chef in the real world.

"We wanted to test our finalists on a wide variety of skills," says co-host/judge Ming Tsai. "Did they have the ability to deliver with few and many resources? To adapt, learn, and think on their feet? And, when pushed to the edge, what did it reveal about their talent, skills, knowledge, and natural ability?"

So as not to overwhelm the finalists right out of the gate, we started with a deceptively simple exercise that proved to be quite revealing: cook an egg in ten minutes. No other instructions, no restrictions. Just an egg and a set amount of time, along with the imagination we hoped they would harness. What we saw that day would continue throughout the competition: great skill, creativity, inspiration, and determination. One of the finalists, Katsuji Tanabe, ended up creating a dessert with his egg. It was something the judges immediately responded to. "He stepped out of the box, which impressed me about this young chef," said co-host/judge Todd English. "And that's one of the qualities that I look for in my kitchen."

As the contest heated up, the finalists were tested on their ability to duplicate someone else's recipe. Celebrated chef Michael Mina joined us in Las Vegas, where he demonstrated one of his signature dishes featuring filet of sole. The finalists were shown only once how to make the dish. A reasonably simple exercise—but it was revealing to see how few of the finalists opted to take notes, the others obviously assuming they could do it from memory. It was also surprising how various the finalists' interpretations of "duplication" turned out to be.

Stepping up the level of challenge, we then tested our finalists on their ability to pair food with wine. After a tour of a splendid wine cellar and a wine tasting with Las Vegas sommelier Martin Heierling, finalists were given the following test: Prepare three distinct appetizers from a kitchen stocked with raw ingredients, and then match each appetizer with appropriate wine. They had only 45 minutes to accomplish this highly demanding assignment.

The challenges demonstrate the skills needed to be a professional chef, but they also teach viewers a thing or two about cooking in their own kitchens; how to pair food with wine, the art of presentation, proper use of salt and other flavorings, timing, and so on. "Even our most seasoned finalists struggled at times with a few of the basics," said co-host/judge Michael Ruhlman. "Right down to the fundamental need to always taste your food and keep your eye on the clock."

The finalists were also being tested in a less overt way—on their endurance. The life of a successful chef demands stamina. The ability to work long hours and put out consistently good meals hour after hour, day after day, is what ultimately separates the stars from the rest of the pack. Unsurprisingly, the process of shooting a reality show duplicates this environment. It calls for optimal performance over extremely long days with very little sleep. Indeed, our reality mirrored the life of a chef. All in all, we were impressed at how well our finalists withstood this test. Our hats go off to them!

Judge Ming Tsai evaluates John Paul Abernathy's dish.

Reflections: Behind the Kitchen Door

Producing *Cooking Under Fire* changed our lives. Heady words, but the creativity, inspiration, determination, and drive we witnessed in the finalists was eye-opening and life-changing. They showed up on Day One not knowing when they would be going home or what the challenge might be. There was never an opportunity to recharge. This boot-camp approach ensured that we challenged them fully. They accepted the conditions without complaint.

We witnessed great attitudes, tremendous professionalism, and a spirit of camaraderie. The twelve finalists competed day in and day out, but their competitive spirit never prevented them from helping each other out. Whether tracking down Indonesian pepper or helping unmold a terrine, they exhibited the special bond that exists among chefs.

Finally, the level of excellence exhibited in the cooking was truly memorable. Not only did it make good television; it reminded us of the caliber of talent out there. It is our hope that *Cooking Under Fire* will deepen the public's understanding of what goes into the making of a chef. A revolution is happening as young chefs graduate from culinary schools and institutes. Food has become hip and fashionable in mainstream America—and it is creative vision and hard work behind the kitchen door that is making that happen.

This series is our tribute to chefs.

W Lance Reynolds
John Rieber
Laurie Donnelly

Finalist Autumn Maddox enjoys a moment of relative quiet at her station.

COOKING UNDER FIRE

Recipes from the Co-Hosts/Judges

Judges Ming, Michael, and Todd are comfortable in the kitchen and at the table.

Pâté de Campagne *serves 10–12 as an appetizer*

Chef Michael Ruhlman

The finalists were asked to prepare a terrine, a skill that co-host/judge Michael Ruhlman considers essential to a great chef. As Michael notes, "All the things that go into great food are combined in this one technique: seasoning, proper cooking times, a good-looking dish. The preparation of terrines gives a good foundation in the knowledge of classic cooking."

The pâté de campagne, or country terrine, is the easiest terrine to make. Distinguished by its coarse rustic texture, the dish calls for a small amount of liver. Use pork liver if it's available to you because it allows for a lower final temperature than chicken liver and therefore produces a moister pâté.

In the spirit of its origins as a humble but delicious dish made from inexpensive cuts of meat, the terrine should be eaten simply, with a baguette and good French Dijon mustard. Add a salad of fresh greens and you've got a delicious simple midweek meal. It's also a fabulous make-ahead dish for a weekend dinner party.

2 pounds fatty boneless pork shoulder butt, cut in 1-inch dice

4 ounces pork or chicken liver

¼ cup chopped white or yellow onion

½ cup coarsely chopped flat-leaf parsley

1-½ tablespoons minced garlic

1 ounce (about 2 tablespoons) kosher salt

Pâté de Campagne

Special equipment: a meat grinder or grinder attachment to a standing mixer, a terrine mold (the recipe is scaled for a 1.5-liter mold), and an instant-read thermometer.

Freeze all your blades and bowls before gathering and measuring your ingredients.

Prepare the Pâté Spice.

Preheat the oven to 300°F. Grind the pork through the large-hole plate of a meat grinder into the bowl of a standing mixer set in ice. Transfer about one-third of the pork to a smaller bowl and add the liver, onion, parsley, garlic, salt, pepper, and pâté spice. Insert the small-hole plate into the grinder, removing any sinew remaining on the blade, and grind the pork-seasonings mixture into the bowl of coarsely ground pork. Refrigerate.

1 teaspoon freshly ground
  black pepper
½ teaspoon pâté spice or quatre
  epices (recipe follows)
2 tablespoons all-purpose flour
2 large eggs
2 tablespoons brandy
½ cup heavy cream
Optional garnish: diced ham,
  cooked mushrooms,
  brine-cured green
  peppercorns (rinsed), duck
  confit (a total of 1 cup)

In a small bowl, combine the flour, eggs, brandy, and cream and stir to blend. This is the *panada,* which helps to bind the pâté. Add it to the ground meat and seasonings. Using the mixer's paddle attachment, mix until the panada is incorporated and the meat becomes sticky, about a minute. (You can also use a wooden spoon or your hands.) Fold in the optional garnish, if using.

Line a 1½-quart terrine mold with plastic wrap, leaving enough overhang on the long sides to fold over the top of the terrine when it's filled. Fill the mold with the pâté mixture, packing it down to remove air pockets. Fold the plastic wrap over the top, and cover with a lid or foil.

Place the terrine in a high-sided roasting pan. Fill with very hot tap water to reach two-thirds up the sides of the terrine mold. Place the pan in the oven and bake until the interior of the terrine reaches 150° F if you are using pork liver, and 160°F if using chicken liver, about an hour.

Remove the pan from the oven. Remove the mold from the waterbath and set a weight of about 2 pounds on top of it. Let cool to room temperature. Refrigerate until completely chilled, overnight or up to 1 week before serving.

1 teaspoon ground clove
1 teaspoon ground nutmeg
1 teaspoon ground ginger
1 teaspoon ground coriander
2 teaspoons ground cinnamon
1 tablespoon ground
  white pepper

Pâté Spice *yields ½ cup*

This is an excellent spice mixture for meat pâtés and terrines.

Quatre épices (four spices) is a similar combination of seasonings—cinnamon, clove, nutmeg and black pepper—that is also good in hearty stews. Quatre épice is typically available in specialty stores. To make it yourself, take the following ingredients:

> 3 tablespoons black peppercorns
> 1 tablespoon fresh ground nutmeg
> 2 teaspoons ground cinnamon
> 2 teaspoons whole cloves

Grind together all spices in a spice mill. Store in an airtight container.

Blue Ginger Crispy Calamari *serves 4*

Chef Ming Tsai

For one of the challenges, finalists had to cook "on the line" in an active restaurant kitchen that was simultaneously serving patrons. Cooking on the line is what the life of a restaurant chef is all about. The finalists watched chefs Todd English and Ming Tsai demonstrate three recipes—Ming's Crispy Calamari and Todd's Bibb Lettuce Salad and Mediterranean Spiced Tuna Loin (recipes follow)—and then worked a half-hour shift on the line preparing the same dishes. Todd English commented, "You can never really refine our craft as much as you'd like. We have to execute it and always think about how it will work on the line. It was interesting to see how these kids did. I learned something by watching them work (the recipes) out in their heads and then try to execute them."

1 teaspoon ground cumin
1 teaspoon ground coriander
1 teaspoon ground fennel
1 teaspoon ground white
  peppercorn
1 tablespoon kosher salt
Canola oil for frying
2 cups Thai Lime Dipping Sauce,
  plus ½ cup for dipping
  (recipe follows)
2 cups all-purpose flour
2 cups sweet-potato flour
  or cornstarch
2 pounds calamari, cleaned and
  cut into ½-inch rings
2 tablespoons thinly sliced
  scallions (white and
  green parts)

Prepare the Thai Lime Dipping Sauce.

In a small frying pan, combine the cumin, coriander, fennel, and white peppercorns. Stir over medium heat until just smoking, 4 to 5 minutes. Cool and transfer to a small serving bowl or ramekin. Add the salt and mix. Set aside.

Fill an electric fryer with the oil to the designated mark, or fill a small stockpot one-third full. Heat the oil to 375°F.

Place a colander in a large bowl into which it just fits and fill the bowl with the Thai Lime Dipping Sauce. In another large bowl, combine the flours.

Working in batches, place the calamari in the first bowl and marinate for 10 seconds. Use the colander to lift the calamari from the bowl and transfer it to the bowl of flour. Using a second colander, dip and lift the calamari in the flours, coating it until no moisture is detectable. Shake the calamari in the colander to remove excess coating.

Transfer the calamari to the oil and fry only until the bubbling sound dies away, 30 to 45 seconds. (The calamari will have turned golden brown.) Using a colander, transfer the calamari to paper towels to drain. Season with the flavored salt, garnish with the scallions, and serve immediately with the dipping sauce.

2 cups Thai fish sauce (nam pla)
3 cups fresh or bottled lime juice
½ cup chopped fresh cilantro
½ cup chopped fresh basil
½ cup chopped fresh mint
1 tablespoon peeled and minced
   fresh ginger

Thai Lime Dipping Sauce *makes about 5 cups*

In a large nonreactive bowl, combine the ingredients. Lasts 1 week, refrigerated.

Tip Mise en place ("put in place") means organization and preparation: before you begin a recipe, measure out all the ingredients. This is the key to making any recipe easy. *Michael Ruhlman*

Bibb Lettuce with a Shower of Roquefort Cheese *serves 4*

Chef Todd English

2 tablespoons walnut oil
⅔ cup chopped walnuts
2 tablespoons fresh lemon juice
    (about ½ lemon)
Splash of balsamic vinegar
2 heads Bibb lettuce, well
    washed, dried, and torn
¼ ordinary white onion, peeled
    and very thinly sliced
1 teaspoon kosher salt
½ teaspoon black pepper
½ cup shaved or crumbled
    Roquefort cheese

Place a small skillet over medium-high heat. When hot, add the oil. Add the walnuts and cook until they are lightly toasted, about 3 minutes. Remove from heat and add the vinegar and lemon juice.

In a large bowl, mix the lettuce and onion. Add salt and pepper. Distribute the lettuce among 4 plates and pour the hot walnut dressing over it. Add the Roquefort cheese and serve immediately.

COOKING
UNDER FIRE

Mediterranean Spiced Tuna Loin *serves 6*

Chef Todd English

2 to 3 pounds sushi or
   #1 tuna loin
6 tablespoons olive oil
Mediterranean Spice Blend
   (recipe follows)
6 tablespoons vegetable oil
1 shallot, roughly chopped
3 tablespoons chopped
   fresh mint
1 cup black olives, pitted
   (kalamata or picholine)
1 cup green olives, pitted
   (cerignola or Sicilian)
2 Calabrese peppers packed
   in oil, drained of excess oil
   and roughly chopped (for
   less heat, you can substitute
   roasted red peppers)
1 tablespoon olive oil

Prepare the Mediterranean Spice Blend.

Trim loins into six 6-inch-long "bricks" (1 inch high and 1 inch wide). Lightly coat one side of each loin with olive oil. Rub the oiled side only with the spice blend until well coated. Heat the vegetable oil in a large sauté pan over medium-high heat. Place the spice-rubbed side of the loins in the pan and sear for approximately one minute or until well browned. Remove from the pan and let rest 3–5 minutes.

In a small bowl, combine shallot, mint, olives, and peppers with enough olive oil to coat and flavor the ingredients.

Freshly ground black pepper
1 tablespoon cardamom
1 tablespoon cumin seeds
1 tablespoon coriander
2 teaspoons cayenne
   pepper flakes
1 tablespoon paprika
1 tablespoon fennel seeds
1 tablespoon turmeric

Mediterranean Spice Blend
Place ingredients in a mortar and pestle and grind until the seeds are well crushed and the ingredients are blended.

Tip For any large fish, such as salmon, tuna, or swordfish, always buy center-cut if you can. It's taken from the part of the fish furthest from the tail, whose flesh is less tender. *Ming Tsai*

Asian Mojo Shrimp *serves 4*

Chef Ming Tsai

1 cup grapeseed or canola oil
2 tablespoons minced garlic
1 tablespoon minced ginger
1 tablespoon minced lemongrass
2 tablespoons minced cilantro
4 Thai bird chiles
1 tablespoon kosher salt
Juice of 3 limes
Kosher salt and freshly ground
    black pepper
20 large shrimp peeled
    and deveined, heads on,
    double-skewered
¼ pound mesclun

Heat the oil until smoking hot. Meanwhile place the next six ingredients in a mortar and pestle and grind to combine. Carefully add the hot oil and stir to "cook." Add the fresh lime juice and season with salt and pepper. Place the skewered shrimp on a tray and smother with the mojo (seasoned oil), reserving ¼ cup to dress salad. Marinate for 30 minutes in the refrigerator.

Season the shrimp with salt and pepper and grill the shrimp skewers on a hot, clean, oiled grill, 3 to 4 minutes per side. (Place the shrimp skewers directly on the grill; do not drain.) While the shrimp cook, continue brushing with mojo. Distribute the greens among 4 plates. Serve shrimp on skewers on top of greens, lightly dressed with mojo.

> ***Tip*** Use a spoon to peel fresh ginger—it's easy and fast, and the spoon's small round tip can get into the nooks. Extra ginger freezes well. You can always have fresh ginger if you store it well-wrapped in the freezer and then grate it frozen as you need it.
> *Michael Ruhlman*

Recipes from the Guest Judges

Guest Chef David Myers of Sona in Los Angeles joins the judges.

Bibb Lettuce and Endive Salad with Pomegranate and Persimmon Dressed in a Toasted Walnut Vinaigrette

serves 4

Chef Govind Armstrong

One of LA's most prominent young chefs, Govind Armstrong of Table 8 is committed to California cuisine using fresh seasonal ingredients from the finest local producers. He has a flair for creating bright and simple dishes without excessive sauces or complicated fusion. For more information, visit www.table8la.com.

2 slices day-old walnut bread

2 tablespoons walnut oil

Kosher salt and freshly ground black pepper

2 heads Bibb lettuce, rinsed and patted dry, outer leaves discarded

2 heads Belgian endive, cores removed, cut crosswise into thin shreds

2 tablespoons fresh flat-leaf parsley leaves

2 ripe Fuyu persimmons, peeled and thinly sliced, preferably with a mandoline

Toasted Walnut Vinaigrette (*recipe follows*)

½ cup pomegranate seeds

¼ cup pomegranate molasses, for serving

Bibb Lettuce and Endive Salad

Prepare the Toasted Walnut Vinaigrette.

Preheat the oven to 350°F. Trim the crusts from the bread. With your fingers, tear into rough pieces; they don't need to be uniform. In a bowl, toss the croutons with 2 tablespoons of walnut oil and season with salt and pepper. Arrange croutons on a sheet pan in a single layer. Bake until the croutons are golden and crisp, about 10 minutes.

In a large mixing bowl, combine the lettuce, endive, and parsley. Dress the salad with about ¼ cup of the Toasted Walnut Vinaigrette and gently toss with your hands to coat evenly.

To serve, arrange the persimmon slices like a fan on 4 plates. Mound a handful of the salad in the center of each plate. Scatter a few croutons and 2 tablespoons of pomegranate seeds on and around each salad. Drizzle the pomegranate molasses around the rim of the dishes. Season with salt and pepper and serve immediately.

COOKING UNDER FIRE

2 minced shallots

2 tablespoons toasted and finely
chopped walnuts

1 teaspoon fresh thyme leaves

2 tablespoons champagne
vinegar

2 tablespoons Spanish sherry
vinegar

¼ cup extra-virgin olive oil

¼ cup grapeseed oil

¼ cup walnut oil

Kosher salt and freshly ground
black pepper

Toasted Walnut Vinaigrette *yields about 1 cup*

Combine the minced shallots, toasted walnuts, and thyme in a mixing bowl. Add the vinegars and whisk to combine. Add the oils in a slow stream, whisking constantly. Season with salt and pepper.

Tip Salt is the most important tool in the kitchen, and the ability to salt food properly is a cook's greatest skill. *Michael Ruhlman*

Grilled Shrimp Tamale with Roasted Poblano, Fava Beans, and Teardrop Tomato Vinaigrette

serves 4 as an appetizer

Chef Frank Randazzo

Frank Randazzo is co-owner and co-chef of Talula in Miami Beach with his wife Andrea Curto-Randazzo. Talula's culinary philosophy draws on both chefs' Italian-American roots and their shared commitment to high-quality fresh ingredients, classic technique, and the extra jolt of Mediterranean-Asian and Southwest flavors. For more information, visit www.talulaonline.com.

4 chopped garlic cloves

3 tablespoons chopped fresh flat-leaf parsley

½ cup plus 1 tablespoon extra-virgin olive oil

16 large shrimp (about 1½ pounds), peeled and deveined

1 poblano pepper

Kosher salt and freshly ground white pepper

1 tablespoon unsalted butter

2 ears sweet corn, kernels cut from the cob (about 1 cup)

½ cup chicken stock

1 ¼ cups heavy cream

¾ cup masa harina

4 dried corn husks (purchased dried), soaked in water until pliable

Teardrop Tomato Vinaigrette (recipe follows)

Grilled Shrimp Tamales

Prepare the Teardrop Tomato Vinaigrette.

Combine the garlic, parsley, and ½ cup oil in a mixing bowl. Add the shrimp, turning to coat them in the marinade. Allow to marinate for 30 minutes to 1 hour.

In the meantime, rub the poblano pepper with the remaining 1 tablespoon of oil. Roast on a very hot grill, over a gas flame, or under a broiler until the skin is blistered and blackened on all sides. Put the poblano in a bowl, cover with plastic wrap, and let sweat for about 10 minutes to loosen the skin. Peel and rub off the charred skin, pull out the core, and remove the seeds. Dice the roasted poblano and set aside.

Place a grill pan over medium-high heat or preheat an outdoor gas or charcoal grill until very hot. Remove the shrimp from the marinade and season with salt and pepper. Lay 8 of the shrimp on the grill and sear 2 minutes per side until the shrimp are firm and pink. Use tongs to remove the grilled shrimp to a side platter.

Chop the remaining 8 shrimp. Place a large sauté pan over medium heat and add butter. When the butter is foamy, add the shrimp, corn, and diced poblano. Sauté for 1 minute. Pour in the chicken stock and cream. Continue to cook until the liquid is reduced slightly and steam rises from the pan. Add the masa harina, reduce the heat to low, and stir for 2 minutes until the mixture thickens. Season with salt and pepper.

Place a corn husk on each of 4 plates. Distribute the sautéed shrimp mixture among the corn-husk "boats." Garnish each tamale with 2 grilled shrimp. Drizzle with 2 tablespoons of Teardrop Tomato Vinaigrette.

½ cup fresh fava beans
½ cup dry white wine, such as Sauvignon Blanc
¼ cup freshly squeezed lemon juice
2 sliced shallots
1 teaspoon whole white peppercorns
1 bay leaf
½ cup (1 stick) cold unsalted butter, cut into small cubes
1 teaspoon tomato paste
2 tablespoons chopped fresh chives
½ cup teardrop tomatoes, halved lengthwise
Kosher salt and freshly ground white pepper

Teardrop Tomato Vinaigrette

Bring a large pot of lightly salted water to a boil. Shell the favas and boil them for 2 minutes. Drain the beans and plunge them into an ice bath to stop the cooking process. Slip off and discard the beans' tough outer skin. Put the beans in a large bowl and set aside.

Place a saucepan over medium-high heat. Pour in the wine and lemon juice. Add the shallots, peppercorns, and bay leaf. Simmer 5 to 10 minutes to reduce the liquid by three-quarters. Whisk in the butter cubes, a few at a time, to emulsify into a velvety sauce. Strain through a fine sieve into a mixing bowl.

Stir in the tomato paste, chives, teardrop tomatoes, and blanched fava beans. Season with salt and white pepper.

Tip Always use kosher or sea salt, not iodized salt. *Michael Ruhlman*

Halibut Poached in Olive Oil with Pickled Shiitakes, Tapioca Pearls, Kaffir Lime Leaf Emulsion, and Indonesian Long Pepper *serves 4*

Chef David Myers

David Myers, chef/owner of the award-winning restaurant Sona in the heart of Los Angeles, embodies the Japanese culinary concept of kappo: *an approach to cooking that emphasizes capturing the exact moment when an ingredient is at its freshest, purest state. David was named* Food & Wine's *Best New Chef of 2003.* Angeleno *magazine voted him Chef of the Year-2004 and he was a finalist for "Rising Star Chef" from the James Beard Foundation. For more information, visit www.sonarestaurant.com.*

4 smashed garlic cloves
4 sprigs fresh thyme
2 Indonesian long peppers
5 cups extra-virgin olive oil
4 6-ounce halibut fillets
Kosher salt and freshly ground
    black pepper
1 lemon
¼ cup minced fresh chives
1 Indonesian long pepper,
    lightly toasted, for garnish
Pickled Shiitakes *(recipe follows)*
Tapioca Pearls *(recipe follows)*
Kaffir Lime Leaf Emulsion
    (recipe follows)

Halibut Poached in Olive Oil

Prepare the Pickled Shiitakes, Tapioca Pearls, and Kaffir Lime Leaf Emulsion.

Place a wide saucepan over medium-low heat. Add the garlic, thyme, 2 Indonesian long peppers, and olive oil. Simmer gently until bubbles appear in the oil, about 145°F.

Season the halibut fillets on both sides with salt and pepper and carefully lay the fish in the oil. Remove from heat and let stand for 20 minutes. Carefully remove the halibut from the oil and pat dry.

Toast the Indonesian long peppers in a DRY pan for two minutes, tossing frequently, until fragrant.

Combine the pickled shiitakes, tapioca, and kaffir lime emulsion in a pot and heat over medium flame until warmed through.

To serve, ladle about ¼ cup of the tapioca, shiitake, and kaffir lime mixture into each of 4 shallow serving bowls. Lay a poached halibut fillet on top. Sprinkle each with a few drops of lemon juice and 1 tablespoon of chives. Using a microplane, grate 4 strokes of toasted Indonesian long pepper on each halibut fillet.

Pickled Shiitakes

1 cup rice vinegar
1 tablespoon sugar
½ pound shiitake mushrooms, wiped of grit and sliced

Combine the vinegar and sugar in a mixing bowl, stirring until the sugar dissolves. Bring a large pot of salted water to a boil over medium-high heat. Add the mushrooms and simmer for 3 minutes until tender. Drain the mushrooms well and add to the vinegar mixture. Cover and allow to cool for 30 to 45 minutes. Remove the mushrooms from the vinegar solution.

Tapioca Pearls

1 cup tapioca pearls
1 quart water

In a saucepan, bring the water to a rolling boil over medium-high heat. Add the tapioca pearls and stir to separate. Reduce the heat to low and simmer until the tapioca becomes translucent, about 15 minutes. Drain the tapioca in a colander and run under cool water.

Kaffir Lime Leaf Emulsion

2 tablespoons sesame oil
2 tablespoons minced fresh ginger
1 tablespoon minced garlic
1 minced scallion, white part only
4 stems fresh cilantro
1 teaspoon whole coriander seeds
½ cup rice vinegar
2 cups unsweetened coconut milk
1 kaffir lime leaf, thinly sliced
2 tablespoons soy sauce
½ lime

Place a sauté pan over medium-low heat and coat with the sesame oil. Add the ginger, garlic, scallion, cilantro stems, and coriander seeds; sauté for 2 minutes until fragrant. Deglaze the pan with the vinegar and reduce the mixture by half. Add the coconut milk and kaffir lime leaf and bring to a boil. Simmer for 20 minutes until thickened and full of flavor. Pour the mixture into a blender and puree until smooth. Strain into a bowl and stir in the soy sauce and lime juice.

Tip Fresh fish should never smell fishy.
Todd English

Phyllo-Crusted Dover Sole with Crab Brandade, Dijon Beurre Blanc, and Haricots Verts *serves 4*

Chef Michael Mina

Award-winning chef Michael Mina's signature dish, Phyllo-Crusted Dover Sole, is featured at his namesake restaurant, MICHAEL MINA Bellagio.

Following a demonstration, the finalists were given 30 minutes to master this elegant dish and reproduce it in the chef's manner. They were judged on taste, overall execution, and presentation, as well as the ability to follow the sequence of steps that compose the dish.

Note: *When making this dish, collect all the components before preparing the fish. For more information, visit www.michaelmina.net.*

½ package phyllo pastry, separated into sheets and laid out overnight to dry
4 fillets Dover sole, skin removed
Kosher salt and freshly ground black pepper
4 large egg whites, beaten
1 cup clarified butter
Crab Brandade *(recipe follows)*
Dijon Beurre Blanc
   (recipe on page 30)
Haricots Verts with Horseradish Cream *(recipe on page 30)*

Phyllo-Crusted Dover Sole

Prepare the Crab Brandade, Haricots Verts with Horseradish Cream, and Dijon Beurre Blanc.

Crush the brittle phyllo sheets into small pieces with your hands. Spread the phyllo crumbs on a shallow platter.

Season the sole on both sides with salt and pepper. Dip the fillets into the beaten egg whites to coat completely, letting the excess drip back into the bowl. Dredge the fish in the crushed phyllo, evenly covering both sides. Press firmly to insure that the crumbs stick.

Heat a large sauté pan over medium heat. Add the clarified butter to the pan. When it begins to smoke, carefully lay 2 fillets in the hot pan. Sauté until golden brown on one side, about 3 minutes. Turn the fish carefully with a spatula and cook the other side for another 3 minutes until a crisp crust forms. Remove to a side plate and repeat with the remaining fillets, adding more butter as needed.

To serve, spoon an oval mound of the Crab Brandade in the center of each plate. Lay a fillet of sole on top. Garnish the fish with a few haricots verts and a dollop of horseradish cream. Drizzle some Dijon beurre blanc around the edge of the plate to finish it.

1 Dungeness crab (about 1½ pounds), live
1 tablespoon vegetable oil
1 sliced yellow onion
2 smashed garlic cloves
1 cup dry white wine, such as Sauvignon Blanc
3 cups heavy cream
1 pound Dungeness crabmeat, picked over for shells
Kosher salt and freshly ground black pepper
8 russet potatoes, peeled

Crab Brandade

For the deepest flavor, it is important to use fresh raw crab. Ask your fishmonger to clean the crab for you. Once the crab is cleaned, it is best to cook it right away. Using a meat mallet, crack the body and legs of the crab.

In a large pot, heat the vegetable oil over a medium flame. When the oil is hazy, add the onion, garlic, and pieces of cracked crab. Sauté until the onion is are translucent, about 3 minutes. Pour in the white wine and cook until its volume is reduced by half, approximately 5 minutes. Add the cream. Turn the heat to low and simmer for 15 to 20 minutes. Strain the crab cream through a fine mesh sieve into another pot and throw away the pieces of crab. Reserve warm.

Meanwhile, put the potatoes in a large pot and cover with cold water. Add 1 tablespoon of salt and bring to a boil uncovered. Simmer until a fork pierces the potatoes easily, about 30 minutes. Drain the potatoes in a colander. While they are still hot, process through a food mill or ricer into a large mixing bowl. Season with salt and pepper.

Stir the crab cream into the potatoes, 1 cup at a time. Continue to combine until the cream is absorbed and the mixture is smooth and creamy. Fold in the crabmeat, breaking it up and distributing it evenly. Adjust seasoning as needed and keep warm.

(continued)

3 sliced shallots

3 thyme sprigs

2 sprigs flat-leaf parsley

1 bay leaf, preferably fresh

1 teaspoon whole black
   peppercorns

1 cup dry white wine, such as
   Sauvignon Blanc

½ cup champagne vinegar

¼ cup heavy cream

¾ pound cold unsalted butter
   cut in chunks

3 tablespoons Dijon mustard

Kosher salt and freshly ground
   black pepper

¼ cup finely chopped fresh
   flat-leaf parsley

Dijon Beurre Blanc

Combine the shallots, thyme, parsley, bay leaf, and peppercorns in a saucepan with the white wine and vinegar. Simmer over medium heat until the liquid is almost totally evaporated.

Stir in the cream and cook until reduced in volume by half. Turn the heat to low and whisk in the butter, 1 or 2 chunks at a time. Continue until all of the butter is incorporated. Whisk in the mustard, taste, and adjust seasoning as needed. Strain the sauce through a fine mesh sieve and keep warm. Stir in chopped parsley just before serving.

½ pound haricots verts (French
   green beans), ends trimmed

3 tablespoons unsalted butter,
   melted

3 tablespoons mascarpone
   cheese

½ tablespoon prepared
   horseradish

Kosher salt and freshly ground
   black pepper

Haricots Verts with Horseradish Cream

Bring a large pot of lightly salted water to a boil. Boil the beans for only 30 seconds. Drain the beans and plunge them into an ice bath to stop the cooking process and preserve their vibrant color. Drain the blanched beans and reserve. Just before serving, heat the beans in the melted butter.

To make the horseradish cream, whip together the mascarpone and horseradish in a small bowl. Season with salt and pepper.

Tip Make sure to salt the water in which you blanch green vegetables. The salt helps them hold their color. Also be sure to have an ice bath ready to "shock" blanched vegetables. It is a myth that ice water "sets" the green color, but it does stop the cooking process, retaining bright color and crisp texture. *Ming Tsai*

COOKING
UNDER FIRE

Grilled Skirt Steak with Citrus Chimichurri, Tostones, and Heart of Palm Salad *serves 4*

Chef Michelle Bernstein

Michelle Bernstein is chef and owner of MB restaurant in Cancun, Mexico, and Miami, Florida. One of the country's most prominent female chefs and restaurateurs, Michelle was named one of South Florida's top chefs by **Ocean Drive**, **Florida International**, *and* **Boca Raton** *magazines. A Miami native, she has created signature dishes featuring the Latin flavors of her childhood blended with Asian, new Caribbean, and classic French influences. Chef Michelle Bernstein is a graduate of Johnson & Wales University, which awarded her an Honorary Doctorate in Culinary Arts in 2003.*

1 to 2 tablespoons olive oil

2 pounds skirt steak, trimmed of excess fat and cut into 4 pieces

Kosher salt and freshly ground black pepper

Citrus Chimichurri
(recipe on page 32)

Heart of Palm Salad
(recipe on page 32)

Tostones *(recipe on page 33)*

Grilled Skirt Steak

Prepare the Citrus Chimichurri, Tostones, and Heart of Palm Salad.

Place a grill pan over medium-high heat or preheat an outdoor gas or charcoal grill until it is very hot. Rub both sides of the steak with oil and season with a generous amount of salt and pepper; the seasoning should be visible on the meat. Grill the steaks for 4 minutes per side, until well-charred on the outside and medium-rare inside. Transfer the steak to a cutting board and let stand for 5 minutes. Cut the steak across the grain on the diagonal and fan the slices out on a platter.

Spoon some Citrus Chimichurri over the meat and pass the remaining sauce at the table. Serve with Tostones and Heart of Palm Salad.

(continued)

> **Tip** Let meat reach room temperature before grilling. *Todd English*

1 cup coarsely chopped
    fresh cilantro
1 cup coarsely chopped
    fresh mint
3 tablespoons rice-wine vinegar
    or white-wine vinegar
2 coarsely chopped garlic cloves
Kosher salt and freshly ground
    black pepper
½ cup extra-virgin olive oil
6 mandarin segments
6 orange segments
3 lime segments
3 lemon segments

Citrus Chimichurri

Combine the herbs, vinegar, garlic, salt, and pepper in a blender. Puree until barely smooth. Pour the herb mixture into a bowl and add the oil and citrus segments; stir to combine. The citrus chimichurri will keep for 4 to 5 days. It is also delicious on seafood and chicken.

2 cups peeled and very thinly
    sliced fresh hearts of palm
6 orange segments, juice
    reserved
4 lime segments, juice reserved
4 lemon segments, juice
    reserved
¼ cup thinly sliced red onions
2 tablespoons coarsely chopped
    cilantro
1 tablespoon seeded and minced
    habanero chile
1 teaspoon sugar
3 tablespoons extra-virgin
    olive oil
Kosher salt and freshly ground
    black pepper

Heart of Palm Salad

In a large bowl, combine the hearts of palm with the fruit segments, onions, cilantro, and habanero. Add the sugar, oil, and juice from the citrus segments. Season well with salt and pepper. Toss the salad gently with your hands and serve. Keeps covered in the refrigerator for up to 3 days.

2 large unripe (green) plantains
½ cup canola oil, for frying
Kosher salt

Tostones (Twice-Fried Plantains)

Peel the plantains and cut into inch-thick slices. In a deep frying pan, heat the oil over medium flame. (You can fry the tostones in one large pan or, if using a smaller pan, in batches.) Fry the plantains until golden-brown and tender, about 2 minutes on each side. Using tongs, transfer the fried plantains to paper towels to drain.

Place the plantain slices on a flat work surface. Press down on each slice firmly with the bottom of a skillet until flattened to about ¼-inch thick. Fry the plantains again for 30 seconds on each side. Transfer to paper towels to drain. Season with salt to taste. Serve immediately.

Yucca-Stuffed Crispy Shrimp with Norman's Mo J., Scotch Bonnet Tartar Salsa, and Hearts of Palm Slaw

serves 4

Chef Norman Van Aken

Norman Van Aken is the chef/owner of the award-winning restaurant NORMAN'S in the historic Coral Gables section of Miami, with sister locations in Orlando and Los Angeles. Norman is the "Father of New World Cuisine" and he coined the term "Fusion Cuisine." For more information, visit www.normans.com.

1 cup boiled and mashed yucca
1 minced Scotch Bonnet chile, stem and seeds discarded
2 or 3 minced garlic cloves
Kosher salt and freshly toasted cracked black pepper, to taste
12 large shrimp (about 1 pound), shell on
1 cup all-purpose flour, seasoned with salt and pepper
1 egg, beaten with 3 tablespoons water to make an egg wash
2 cups panko (Japanese bread crumbs)
Peanut oil for frying
Scotch Bonnet Tartar Salsa
   (recipe follows)
Norman's Mo J. *(recipe follows)*
Hearts of Palm Slaw
   (recipe on page 36)

Yucca-Stuffed Crispy Shrimp

Prepare the Scotch Bonnet Tartar Salsa, Norman's Mo J., and Hearts of Palm Slaw.

In a mixing bowl, combine the mashed yucca with the chile, garlic, salt, and pepper and set aside.

Peel and devein the shrimp leaving the tail on. Butterfly the shrimp by cutting lengthwise almost all the way through from inside the curl. Open up the shrimp to resemble a butterfly and pat dry with paper towels. Stuff about ¾ tablespoon of the yucca mash into the cavity of each shrimp, packing it firmly into place. Dredge the stuffed shrimp lightly in the flour. Dip into the egg wash and then the panko. Repeat with remaining shrimp. Set aside on a plate.

In a large heavy pot, heat 3 inches of peanut oil until very hot (350°F). Fry the shrimp in the hot oil for 2 minutes until golden and cooked through. Remove to a paper-towel-lined platter.

To serve, put a small mound of the Hearts of Palm Slaw on the center of each plate. Spoon a small dollop of the Scotch Bonnet Tartar Salsa onto each plate, just off-center. Rest 3 shrimp on top of the salsa and drizzle Mo J. directly onto each shrimp.

COOKING UNDER FIRE

3 large egg yolks
1 tablespoon champagne vinegar
1 teaspoon pickling juice from
Pickled Scotch Bonnets
(recipe follows)
½ cup extra-virgin olive oil
½ cup canola oil
1½ tablespoons pickled Scotch
Bonnet chiles (recipe follows)
3 tablespoons finely diced sweet
butter pickles
2 tablespoons finely diced
red onion
1 hard-cooked large egg, yolk
sieved, white chopped small
Kosher salt and freshly cracked
black pepper

Scotch Bonnet Tartar Salsa

Put the egg yolks in a blender and whip until pale yellow. With the motor running, add the vinegar and pickling juice. Once blended, slowly drizzle in the olive and canola oils in a steady stream until thickened.

Remove the mixture to a bowl and add the pickled chiles, sweet butter pickles, and red onion. Stir in the hard-cooked egg. Season to taste with salt and pepper. Keep covered and refrigerated until needed.

8 ounces whole Scotch Bonnet
chiles, stem on and seeds
intact
6 thinly sliced garlic cloves
1 tablespoon whole mustard
seeds
1 tablespoon dill seeds
6 small bay leaves
1 cup apple-cider vinegar
1 cup champagne vinegar
1 cup water

Pickled Scotch Bonnets

Cut a small, thin slit in each Scotch Bonnet. Place the chiles and garlic in a glass bowl and set aside.

Combine the mustard seeds, dill seeds, bay leaves, vinegars, and water in a saucepan and bring to a boil over medium heat. Pour the mixture over the chiles and garlic, and weigh them down with a plate so they are completely submerged. Let cool to room temperature. Transfer the pickled chiles and liquid to an airtight jar or container and keep refrigerated up to 1 month.

6 minced garlic cloves
1 or 2 minced Scotch Bonnet
chiles, stem and seeds
discarded
½ teaspoon kosher salt
2 teaspoons toasted
cumin seeds
1 cup extra-virgin olive oil
⅓ cup sour/blood orange juice
2 teaspoons Spanish
sherry vinegar
Kosher salt and freshly ground
black pepper

Norman's Mo J. *makes 1¼ cups*

Mash the garlic, chiles, salt, and cumin together in a mortar until fairly smooth. Scrape into a mixing bowl and set aside.

In a small pot, heat the olive oil until fairly hot. Pour over the garlic-chile mixture and let stand for 10 minutes. Whisk in the sour orange juice and vinegar. Season with salt and pepper to taste. Set aside at room temperature until ready to use.

(continued)

1 ½ cups fresh hearts of palm, peeled and very thinly sliced

¼ cup peeled and julienned jicama

¼ red bell pepper, stem and seeds discarded, julienned

¼ yellow bell pepper, stem and seeds discarded, julienned

1 Scotch Bonnet chile, stem and seeds discarded, minced

½ small red onion, julienned

3 scallions, white and green parts, finely chopped

½ cup extra-virgin olive oil

¼ cup freshly squeezed orange juice

1 teaspoon freshly toasted and ground coriander seed

½ teaspoon sugar

½ teaspoon freshly ground black pepper

Kosher salt to taste

Hearts of Palm Slaw

Mix the hearts of palm, jicama, bell peppers, Scotch Bonnet chile, onion, and scallions in a large bowl and set aside.

In another bowl, mix the olive oil, orange juice, coriander, sugar, pepper, and salt until well blended. Pour the dressing over the slaw and mix to combine.

COOKING UNDER FIRE

Recipes from the Finalists

Finalists Yannick Marchand, Jennifer McDermott and Matt Leeper shave, dice, and slice.

Grilled Radicchio and Endive Bruschetta with Aged Balsamic Vinegar and Shaved Pecorino

serves 4 as cicchetti (*Venetian snacks, similar to tapas*)

Chef William Barlow

"*I was inspired to develop this recipe when I visited California to appear on the show,*" explains chef Barlow. "*Serve it as a starter. Any kind of cured meat turns this dish into a light lunch.*"

¼ to ½ cup fruity extra-virgin olive oil

1 large head radicchio, halved through the core

2 heads Belgian endive, halved lengthwise

Kosher salt and freshly ground black pepper

1 tablespoon minced shallots

2 tablespoons chopped fresh flat-leaf parsley

¼ cup good-quality balsamic vinegar

4 slices ciabatta bread, about 1 inch thick

2-ounce wedge pecorino cheese

Place a grill pan over medium-high heat or preheat an outdoor gas or charcoal grill until very hot. Rub a tablespoon or so of oil on the radicchio and endive to prevent it from sticking. Place the radicchio and endive on the grill, cut side down, and season with salt and pepper. Sear until the bottoms begin to char and wilt slightly, about 3 minutes. Turn over and sear the other side until tender, about 2 minutes more. Transfer the grilled radicchio and endive to a bowl, cover tightly with plastic wrap, and allow to steam until it reaches room temperature, about 20 minutes.

Remove the radicchio and endive from the bowl and core them. Thinly slice both crosswise into shreds and put into a bowl. Add the shallots, parsley, and half the balsamic vinegar; season with salt and pepper. Drizzle with a couple of tablespoons of oil and set aside at room temperature to marinate.

In the meantime, brush both sides of the bread slices with oil and season with salt and pepper. Grill until the bread is crisp and golden, about 5 minutes. Top the toasted bread with the lettuce mixture. Using a vegetable peeler, shave large curls of cheese over the bruschetta. Finish with a drizzle of the remaining balsamic.

Infused French Goat Cheese Wrapped in a Phyllo Purse *serves 4 as an appetizer*

Chef Russell Moore

½ cup balsamic vinegar
1 6-ounce log goat cheese, at room temperature
¼ cup sugar
Pinch of ground cinnamon
Pinch of ground nutmeg
⅛ teaspoon freshly squeezed lemon juice
1 small yellow onion
1 medium Granny Smith apple
2 tablespoons clarified butter
1 teaspoon whole fennel seed
Kosher salt and freshly ground black pepper
3 sheets of phyllo pastry, thawed
2 large eggs beaten with 2 tablespoons water to make an egg wash

In a small pot, heat the balsamic vinegar over a medium flame. Cook until it reaches the consistency of molasses and slightly less than half its original volume, about ¼ cup. Remove from heat and set aside to cool.

In a mixing bowl, thoroughly blend the goat cheese, sugar, cinnamon, nutmeg, and lemon juice. Set aside.

Peel the onion and dice it finely. Peel and core the apple and dice finely. Heat a large sauté pan over medium flame and coat with the clarified butter. When the butter is hot, add the onion and apple. Turn down the heat to low. Sauté 5 to 8 minutes until the onions and apples are caramelized (golden-brown, not burned). Sprinkle in the fennel seeds, tossing to combine. After about 20 seconds, fold this hot mixture into the goat-cheese mixture, blending to incorporate. Season with salt and pepper to taste. Chill in the refrigerator for at least 20 minutes.

Unroll the phyllo pastry and lay one sheet flat on a clean cleared work surface. Cover the 2 unused sheets with a damp (not wet) cloth to prevent them from becoming brittle. Cut the phyllo sheet into 4 squares. Place a dollop of the goat-cheese mixture in the center of each square. Brush the egg wash around 3 sides of the mixture, leaving one side dry (it will become the flower at the top of the purse). Gather up the 4 corners of the phyllo square around the goat-cheese filling, twist, and crimp together to form a little package or purse. Repeat the procedure with the remaining 2 sheets of phyllo.

Preheat the oven to 350°F. Coat a sheet pan with nonstick cooking spray. Place the phyllo purses on the pan and bake approximately 10 to 15 minutes or until crisp and golden.

To serve, drizzle 1 tablespoon of the balsamic reduction on each of 4 plates. Arrange 3 hot goat-cheese purses on each plate.

Spicy Sweet-and-Sour Shrimp with Watercress

serves 4 as an appetizer

Chef Yannick Marchand

Yannick suggests pairing his appetizer with a crisp Pinot Grigio or a French white wine such as Sancerre, Loire.

8 large unshelled shrimp
   (about ¾ pound), head on
1 diced onion
1 diced carrot
1 diced celery stalk
5 fresh flat-leaf parsley sprigs
3 fresh thyme sprigs
2 bay leaves
½ cup apple-cider vinegar,
   preferably organic
½ cup sugar, preferably organic
Pinch of cayenne
1 vanilla bean, split lengthwise
   and scraped
Sea salt and freshly ground
   black pepper
Extra-virgin olive oil
1 bunch watercress, stems
   trimmed, rinsed and dried
Juice of ½ lime

Remove the shrimp heads and shells and reserve. Devein each shrimp and set aside.

Place a dry saucepan over a medium-high flame until hot. Add the shrimp heads and shells and cook for a minute or two (without liquid). Add the mirepoix (onion, carrot, and celery) and the parsley, thyme, and bay leaves. Continue to cook and stir until the vegetables soften a bit and smell good.

Raise the heat to high and add cold water to cover. Bring to a boil, then lower the heat and simmer gently for 30 minutes, skimming off any impurities that rise to the surface. Strain the shrimp stock through a fine mesh sieve to remove the solids.

In a small saucepan over medium flame, whisk the vinegar and sugar together. Simmer and continue whisking until the sugar dissolves and the mixture reduces to a thick syrup, about 5 minutes. Pour in the shrimp stock and continue to simmer until reduced to the consistency of a sauce. Season with cayenne, vanilla, salt, and ground pepper. Remove from the heat and hold warm.

Coat a large nonstick skillet with oil and place over medium heat. Season the shrimp on all sides with salt and pepper. Sauté the shrimp in the hot oil for 2 to 4 minutes until pink and firm.

Put the watercress in a bowl. Drizzle with 2 tablespoons of olive oil and the lime juice. Season with salt and pepper and toss gently with your hands.

To serve, place a small mound of watercress on each of 4 plates. Lay 2 shrimp on top. Drizzle the sauce on the shrimp and around the rim of the plates.

Pear-Fennel Salad with Roquefort Vinaigrette

serves 4 as an appetizer

Chef Sara Lawson

2 large fennel bulbs shaved paper-thin, preferably on a mandoline
1 teaspoon fennel fronds
2 ripe pears, thinly sliced
Kosher salt and freshly ground black pepper
½ cup crumbled Roquefort cheese
2 tablespoons minced fresh chives

Pear-Fennel Salad

Prepare the Roquefort Vinaigrette.

In a mixing bowl, combine the fennel slices, fennel fronds, and pears; season with salt and pepper. Dress the salad with ¼ cup of the vinaigrette and gently toss with your hands to combine. Divide the salad among 4 plates. Garnish each with 2 tablespoons of Roquefort and a sprinkling of chives.

1 minced shallot
¼ cup crumbled Roquefort cheese
1 teaspoon freshly squeezed lemon juice
¼ cup champagne vinegar
1 cup extra-virgin olive oil
Kosher salt and freshly ground black pepper

Roquefort Vinaigrette

Put the minced shallots and cheese in a mixing bowl. Add the lemon juice and vinegar and whisk to combine. Add the oil in a slow stream, whisking constantly. Season with salt and pepper.

Tip Your knife is your most important tool. Make sure it is always properly sharpened. *Todd English*

Shiitake Mushroom Tart with Duck Confit and Soft Poached Egg *serves 4 as an appetizer*

Chef Autumn Maddox

For a complete meal, serve with a small salad dressed with whole-grain mustard vinaigrette.

2 duck legs

Kosher salt and freshly ground black pepper

¾ cup (1½ sticks) unsalted butter

½ yellow onion, thinly sliced

1 pound shiitake mushrooms, wiped of grit, stems trimmed, thinly sliced

2 minced garlic cloves

1 cup heavy cream

½ cup dry white wine, such as Sauvignon Blanc

2 large egg yolks, beaten with 2 tablespoons water to make an egg wash

4 large eggs

Filling

Prepare the Pâté Brisée.

Preheat the oven to 450°F. Season the duck legs heavily with salt and pepper. In a cast-iron skillet, roast the duck legs skin side up for 1 hour, basting every 15 minutes with the fat that accumulates. Remove the duck legs from the oven, shred, and reserve the crisp duck skin for garnish on top of tart.

Place a sauté pan over medium-high heat and add half the butter. When the butter is melted, add the onions and season with salt and pepper. Sauté until the onions release their moisture and caramelize, about 3 minutes. Remove from heat and cool to room temperature.

Place a clean skillet over medium heat and add the remaining butter. When the butter is melted, add the mushrooms and season with salt and pepper. Sauté for 3 minutes until the mushrooms begin to brown. Add the garlic and sauté 1 minute more. Remove from the heat, taste, and adjust salt and pepper if needed. Allow to cool.

Preheat the oven to 375°F. Lightly dust a work surface with flour. Roll out the dough thinly and punch out four 6-inch circles using a ring mold. Spoon one-quarter of the mushroom mixture in the center of each round, leaving a border all around. (The border should be wide enough to almost reach the center when folded.) Top the mushrooms with one-quarter of the caramelized onions and a scattering of the duck confit. Brush the dough border with the egg wash. Fold the border of the dough over the filling, leaving it exposed in the center. (This is a free-form rustic tart; it does not have to look perfect.) Gently fold and pinch the dough to seal any cracks. Brush

the top and sides of the dough with the remaining egg wash. Using your hands or a spatula, place the tarts on a sheet pan lined with parchment paper. Bake 25 to 30 minutes until nicely browned.

When the tarts are within ten minutes of being done, begin cooking the eggs. Fill a wide pot with 3 inches of water. Add 1 teaspoon salt and bring to a gentle simmer over medium-high heat. Carefully crack the eggs into the simmering water, spacing them apart. Poach for 3 minutes until barely cooked, making sure the yolks are still soft. Remove the poached eggs with a slotted spoon and dab the bottom with a paper towel to blot dry. Place a poached egg on top of each mushroom tart, season with salt and pepper, and serve.

1 ¼ cups all-purpose flour, plus extra for dusting
½ teaspoon kosher salt
½ cup (1 stick) cold unsalted butter, cut in cubes
3 to 5 tablespoons ice water

Pâté Brisée

Chill all the ingredients, as well as the bowl and blade of a food processor.

Add the flour and salt to the food processor fitted with the chilled blade; pulse to combine. Add the butter, a few cubes at a time, pulsing until the mixture resembles small peas. Add ice water, a bit at a time, until the dough starts to come together without being wet or sticky. Pinch a small amount together; if it is crumbly, add more ice water a teaspoon at a time. Form the dough into a disk and wrap in plastic wrap. Refrigerate for at least 1 hour.

Tip Scales are an inexpensive but very valuable cooking tool. For the most accurate and consistent results when baking, use a scale to weigh dry ingredients. *Michael Ruhlman*

Snapper Ceviche with Key West Flavors and Yucca Chips *serves 4 as an appetizer*

Chef Autumn Maddox

½ pound red snapper fillets,
    boneless and skinless,
    ½ inch dice
5 Key limes, zested and juiced
2 Valencia oranges, zested
    and juiced
¼ cup rice vinegar
2 minced garlic cloves
1 jalapeño, seeded and
    diced small
Kosher salt and freshly ground
    black pepper
1 ripe mango, halved, pitted,
    peeled, and diced small
2 tablespoons coarsely chopped
    fresh cilantro plus more
    for garnish
Yucca chips for serving
    (recipe follows)

Snapper Ceviche

Place the diced snapper in a large mixing bowl. Add the zest and juice of the Key limes and oranges. Add the rice vinegar, garlic, and jalapeño; season with salt and pepper. Toss gently and refrigerate covered for 1 hour to "cook" the fish in the acid.

Fold the mango and cilantro into the ceviche. Taste and adjust seasoning as needed. Using a slotted spoon, scoop the ceviche onto 4 small chilled plates or martini glasses. Garnish with fresh cilantro. Serve with freshly fried Yucca Chips on the side (and a shot of tequila).

Peanut or vegetable oil, for frying
1 pound fresh yucca

Yucca Chips

Heat 3 inches of oil in a large heavy pot or deep fryer to 375°F.

While the oil is heating, peel the yucca. Using a mandoline or a very sharp knife, slice the yucca so thinly that you can see through each slice. Submerge the slices of yucca in a bowl of cold water for 2 minutes.

Drain the yucca in a colander; shake gently to remove excess water. One at a time, drop the yucca chips into the hot oil and fry until crisp for about 1 minute; do not brown. Using a slotted spoon, remove the yucca chips to a platter lined with paper-towels. While the chips are still hot, season with a light sprinkling of salt.

Caramelized Apple Ravioli with Rosemary Caramel and Cardamom Yogurt *serves 4 as an appetizer*

Chef Autumn Maddox

2 cups sugar plus 2 tablespoons
2 tablespoons toasted and
  ground cardamom pods
1 cup plain whole-milk yogurt
2 tablespoons honey
1 cup (2 sticks) unsalted butter
2 Fuji apples, peeled, cored,
  and thinly sliced
2 Granny Smith apples, one
  peeled, cored, and thinly
  sliced, the other left whole
1 teaspoon ground cinnamon
Kosher salt
½ cup heavy cream
1 fresh rosemary sprig
1 large sheet fresh pasta,
  about 11 by 14 inches
1 large egg beaten with 1
  tablespoon water to make
  an egg wash
Canola oil for frying

In a small bowl, combine 2 tablespoons of sugar with ½ tablespoon of the cardamom and set aside.

In a mixing bowl, combine the yogurt, honey, and remaining 1½ tablespoons of ground cardamom. Mix and season with salt to taste. Put half the cardamom yogurt in a container and freeze. Refrigerate the remaining yogurt.

Place a sauté pan over medium heat and add half the butter. When the butter begins to foam, toss in the apple slices, ½ cup sugar, and the cinnamon. Cook and stir until golden brown; season with salt. When the apples have some color and are tender, remove from the heat. Set aside to cool to room temperature.

In a large pot, combine the remaining 1½ cups sugar and ½ cup cool water; the mixture should look like wet sand. Bring to a boil over medium heat and watch closely for the color to change. When the sugar caramelizes and reaches a golden amber hue, remove from heat. Stir in the remaining ½ cup of butter and the cream. Return to medium heat, bring to a simmer, and cook for 4 minutes until smooth. Remove from heat, add the sprig of rosemary, and hold in a warm place.

To form the ravioli, cut the pasta sheet into 4 equal squares. Spoon one-quarter of the apple mixture in the center of each square and brush the edges with the egg wash. Fold the top right corner down to meet the bottom left corner, forming a triangle. Press the edges firmly with your fingers to make a tight seal. Repeat with the other 3 squares.

(continued)

Heat 3 inches of oil in a large heavy pot or deep fryer to 375°F. Fry the ravioli in batches until they float and are golden brown, about 3 to 4 minutes. Using a slotted spoon, remove the ravioli from the oil and drain on a paper-towel-lined plate. Lightly dust with the reserved cardamom sugar.

Puddle the caramel sauce on 4 small plates, then add a dollop of the chilled cardamom yogurt. Nestle a warm ravioli on top and garnish with a scoop of the frozen cardamom yogurt. With a microplane or box grater, grate some of the Granny Smith apple, skin and all, over the top and serve.

COOKING
UNDER FIRE

Marcona Almond-Crusted Foie Gras with Pluot Glaze

serves 4 as an appetizer

Chef Sara Lawson

1½ cups Marcona almonds
4 3-ounce slices of Grade A
  foie gras, cleaned
Kosher salt and freshly ground
  black pepper
3 tablespoons canola oil
2 tablespoons unsalted butter
2 ripe pluots or young plums,
  pitted and sliced into
  thin wedges
½ pound baby arugula
Pluot Glaze *(recipe follows)*

Marcona Almond-Crusted Foie Gras

Prepare the Pluot Glaze.

Finely grind the almonds in a mini-chopper or food processor and spread out on a platter. Preheat the broiler.

Season the foie gras medallions on both sides with salt and pepper and place on a baking pan in a single layer. Broil the foie gras for about 20 seconds, just until it begins to melt. Lay the medallions in the ground almonds, broiled side down, so the almonds stick and form a crust.

Place a sauté pan over medium-high heat. Film the pan with 1 tablespoon of oil. When the oil is hot, add the foie gras medallions to the pan, crust side down. Sear for 1 minute; then carefully turn them with a spatula and sear the other side for 1 minute. Remove from heat.

Place a sauté pan over medium heat and add the butter. When the butter is foamy, add the plums and sauté for 2 minutes until warmed through; season with salt and pepper.

Put the arugula in a mixing bowl and coat with the remaining 2 tablespoons of oil. Season with salt and pepper and toss gently with your hands.

To serve, mound a handful of the arugula on each of 4 plates. Lean one medallion of almond-crusted foie gras on the greens, arrange the pluot wedges around the plate, and drizzle with warm pluot glaze.

3 ripe pluots or young plums,
  pitted, pureed, and strained
½ cup sugar
Dash of cayenne
Dash of salt

Pluot Glaze

Combine the plum juice and sugar in a saucepan and place over medium heat. Cook for 5 minutes until syrupy. Stir in the cayenne and salt.

Simple Poached Eggs with Tomato Brunoise and Parsley Garnish *serves 4*

Chef Jennifer McDermott

2 tablespoons white vinegar
4 large eggs
1 large Roma tomato, finely diced
¼ cup fresh flat-leaf parsley leaves
Kosher salt and freshly ground black pepper

Fill a wide pot or deep skillet with 3 inches of water. Add the vinegar and bring to a simmer over medium-high heat. When the water is barely bubbling, gently crack one of the eggs into a small measuring cup, taking care not to break it. Carefully slide the egg into the simmering water. (Be careful not to let the water reach a rolling boil when adding the egg; the egg will fall apart.) Repeat with the remaining eggs, spacing them apart; it is fine to cook 2 eggs at a time. Poach until the white is completely cooked but the yolks are still slightly runny, 3 to 4 minutes.

Remove the poached eggs with a slotted spoon. Dab the bottom of each egg with a paper towel to dry. Set each poached egg on a small plate. Scatter diced tomato on top of the egg and around the plate. Garnish each dish with a few parsley leaves; season with salt and pepper to taste.

"Japsican" Tempura with Sour Orange Ponzu *serves 4*

Chef Katsuji Tanabe

"Being Japanese and Mexican, I have grown up loving the flavors from both cuisines. So I thought: why not bring them together?" says chef Tanabe. "The sour orange from South Mexico, the Ponzu sauce from Japan, the fish and fruits (as well as the tempura style of cooking) from the Gulf of Mexico."

Peanut or canola oil,
    for deep frying
½ cup rice flour
½ cup all-purpose flour
¼ cup cornstarch, plus more
    for dredging
1 tablespoon paprika
3 tablespoons kosher salt,
    plus more for seasoning
1 tablespoon freshly ground
    black pepper, plus more
    for seasoning
Ice-cold water or seltzer, as
    needed (about 1½ cups)
2 Florida avocadoes, halved,
    pitted, peeled, and sliced
1 small papaya, halved, seeded,
    peeled, and sliced
8 ounces red snapper fillet,
    cut in 4 even pieces

Tempura

Prepare the Sour Orange Ponzu.

Heat about 3 inches of oil in a large heavy pot or deep fryer to 375°F. While the oil is heating, mix the flours, cornstarch, paprika, salt, and pepper in a large bowl. Whisk in the ice water until the consistency resembles pancake batter consistency is achieved and there are no lumps.

Spread about 1 cup of cornstarch on a shallow plate. Dust the slices of avocado, papaya, and fish in the cornstarch, shaking off the excess. Dip the fruit and fish fillets in the batter with a slotted spoon one by one to coat lightly but completely, letting the excess drip back into the bowl. Gently lower them into the hot oil in batches; do not overcrowd the pot. The tempura should "fizz" when the tempura hit the hot oil. Fry for 2 minutes; then use tongs or chopsticks to turn the pieces so they cook evenly. When the coating is light golden-brown and crisp, carefully remove the tempura to a plate lined with paper towels. While the tempura is still hot, lightly season with salt and pepper. Arrange the tempura on a plate and serve with Sour Orange Ponzu sauce for dipping.

1 cup soy sauce
½ cup sour orange juice
1 tablespoon finely minced
    fresh ginger

Sour Orange Ponzu

Combine the soy sauce, sour orange juice, and ginger in a bowl. Whisk until well combined.

Purple Thai "Risotto" with Sausage Ratatouille *serves 4*

Chef Blair King

¼ cup rendered duck fat
    or unsalted butter
1 minced shallot
1½ cups purple Thai rice
1 cup dry white wine,
    such as Chablis
Prawn Poaching Liquid
    (recipe follows)
6 fresh basil leaves, chopped
Kosher salt and freshly ground
    black pepper
1 cup coarsely grated
    Parmigiano-Reggiano

Purple Thai "Risotto"

Prepare the Prawn Poaching Liquid.

Place a large sauté pan over medium heat and add the duck fat or butter. When the fat begins to smoke, add the shallot. Cook and stir for 5 minutes until translucent. Add the rice and stir for 1 or 2 minutes until the grains begin to pop and are slightly toasted.

Add the wine and cook until almost totally evaporated. Pour in 1 cup of the warm Prawn Poaching Liquid. Stir with a wooden spoon until the rice has absorbed all the liquid; then add another cup. Keep stirring while adding poaching liquid 1 cup at a time, allowing the rice to absorb it before adding more. The rice will be a vibrant purplish-red.

Taste the risotto; it should be slightly firm but creamy—neither mushy nor raw. Add the basil and season with salt and pepper. Remove from the heat and fold in the parmesan.

2 cups shrimp shells
1 quart cold water
2 cups dry white wine,
    such as Chablis
8 kaffir lime leaves
3 Indonesian long peppers,
    coarsely chopped
2 tablespoons kosher salt

Prawn Poaching Liquid

Put the shrimp shells in a stockpot and add only enough cold water to cover by 2 inches, about 1 quart. Add the wine and slowly bring to a simmer, uncovered, over medium heat. Skim off any impurities that rise to the surface.

When the liquid reaches a boil, reduce the heat to a simmer and toss in the kaffir lime leaves, Indonesian long pepper, and salt. Simmer gently for 30 minutes. Strain the liquid into another container and discard the solids. Hold warm.

2 tablespoons extra-virgin
 olive oil
4 spicy sausages, sliced
 ¼-inch thick
1 yellow onion, finely diced
1 red bell pepper, cored
 and diced
1 green bell pepper, cored
 and diced
½ Italian eggplant, unpeeled,
 ¼ inch dice
Kosher salt and freshly ground
 black pepper
2 chopped garlic cloves
1 small zucchini, diced
1 tomato, unpeeled, seeded
 and chopped
2 teaspoons fresh thyme leaves
2 teaspoons fresh
 oregano leaves
2 teaspoons chopped fresh
 rosemary needles
1 bay leaf
¼ cup dry white wine,
 such as Chablis
2 tablespoons good-quality
 balsamic vinegar

Sausage Ratatouille

Place a large sauté pan over medium heat and coat with the oil. When the oil gets hazy, add the sausage medallions and sear on both sides until cooked through. Using tongs or a slotted spoon, remove the cooked sausage to a platter. There should be plenty of rendered pork fat left the pan.

Add the onion, bell peppers, and eggplant to the fat and sauté for 5 minutes until the vegetables soften; season with salt and pepper. Toss in the garlic, zucchini, tomato, and herbs. Cook, stirring occasionally, until tender, about 7 minutes. Deglaze with the wine and balsamic vinegar. Return the sausage to the pan and toss to combine. Season with salt and pepper to taste.

Sautéed Shrimp with Shiitakes, Duck Cracklings, and Citrus Ponzu *serves 4*

Chef John Paul Abernathy

"I used 5 prawns as it is bad luck in Eastern culture to serve 4 portions. We only want good luck when eating, so please adjust your numbers accordingly," says chef Abernathy.

1 cup duck skin (*see Note*)
Kosher salt
16 large shrimp (about 1½ pounds), head and shell on
½ teaspoon ground Indonesian long pepper, toasted
1 pound shiitake mushrooms, wiped of grit, stems trimmed
Citrus Ponzu (*recipe follows*)

Note: *Cut off a handful of fatty skin from a duck. Particularly good is the stubby tail of skin that protrudes from the cavity, known as "the pope's nose."*

Sautéed Shrimp

Prepare the Citrus Ponzu.

Slice the duck skin and fat into small strips. Place a heavy-bottomed saucepan over medium heat. When the pan is hot, add the duck skin. Cook until crisp, about 6 minutes. Using tongs or a slotted spoon, remove the fried bits from the pan and drain on a paper-towel-lined plate. Season the cracklings with salt while still hot and set aside. Set the saucepan aside; there should be ample fat left in the bottom.

Carefully remove the heads of the shrimp in one piece and set aside. (Fried shrimp heads are delicious. If you are too squeamish to eat them, save them for a shrimp stock.) Peel the shrimp and discard the shells. Devein the shrimp. Season the shrimp with salt and ground long pepper.

Place 2 sauté pans over medium heat. Film each pan with about 1 tablespoon of the reserved duck fat. Sauté the shiitakes in one pan until they release their moisture and brown slightly. In the other pan, sauté the shrimp for 4 minutes or until they curl and are firm to the touch. (Meanwhile, if you are game to serve shrimp heads, place the saucepan of remaining duck fat over medium heat. Fry the shrimp heads until barely brown.)

To serve, line a platter or 4 plates with a bed of sautéed shiitakes. Scatter a few duck cracklings around. Arrange the shrimp, alternately with the shrimp heads, on top. Drizzle Citrus Ponzu over the plate.

1 cup soy sauce
⅓ cup mirin
¼ cup rice vinegar
¼ cup freshly squeezed
    orange juice
zest of one orange, finely grated

Citrus Ponzu

In a small saucepan, combine the soy sauce, mirin, and vinegar. Place over medium heat and gently bring to a simmer; do not boil. When the liquid starts to bubble, remove from heat and add the orange juice and zest. Allow to cool to room temperature.

Blackened Center-Cut Pork Chops with Dirty Rice

serves 4

Chef Michael Duronslet

¼ cup kosher salt
1 tablespoon cayenne
1 tablespoon chili powder
1 teaspoon granulated garlic
1 teaspoon granulated onion
½ teaspoon paprika
½ teaspoon ground cumin
½ teaspoon white pepper
Pinch of ground coriander
¼ cup canola oil, plus more
    for coating the chops
4 12-ounce bone in center-cut
    pork chops
Dirty Rice *(recipe follows)*

Blackened Center-Cut Pork Chops

Prepare the Dirty Rice.

Preheat the oven to 350°F. To make the rub, combine the salt and spices in a wide shallow bowl and mix to distribute evenly.

Rub both sides of the pork chops with a little oil and press into the spice rub to coat evenly.

Place a large cast-iron skillet over medium heat and add 2 tablespoons of the oil. When white smoke appears, lay 2 pork chops in the pan and brown for about 30 seconds per side. (The spices should just form a crust, not burn.) Remove the seared pork chops to a large baking pan. Coat the skillet with the remaining 2 tablespoons of oil and sear the remaining 2 chops. Add them to the baking pan.

Put the baking pan in the oven and roast the chops for about 20 minutes. The pork is done when the center is still rosy and the internal temperature reads 145°F when tested with an instant-read thermometer.

To serve, pack the dirty rice into a small ramekin and turn it over onto a plate to form a tidy mound. Lean a pork chop against the rice mound with the bone facing up. Repeat with the remaining 3 portions.

COOKING UNDER FIRE

2 pounds ground beef
½ pound ground pork
¼ pound beef liver, cubed
Kosher salt and freshly ground
     black pepper
1 medium onion, finely chopped
5 minced garlic cloves
1 green bell pepper, finely
     chopped
4 cups cooked white rice, hot
Juice of 3 or 4 blood oranges
¼ cup slivered almonds,
     lightly toasted

Dirty Rice

Place a large sauté pan over medium heat. When the pan is hot, add the ground beef, pork, and liver; season with salt and pepper. Cook and stir for 5 minutes until a fair amount of fat appears in the pan and the meat begins to brown.

Add the onion, garlic, and bell pepper; season again with salt and pepper. Continue to cook for 10 minutes until the vegetables are soft and the meat is completely cooked. Season again with salt and pepper. Tip out any excess oil and hold warm.

In a large bowl, combine the rice with the orange juice and carefully fold in the meat mixture. Add the almonds and toss to combine.

Ancho- and Pepita-Crusted Beef Medallions with Potatoes Anna, Sautéed Pluots, and Red-Wine Reduction *serves 4*

Chef Matthew Leeper

1 cup salted pepitas
 (green pumpkin seeds)
2 ancho chiles, stemmed,
 seeded, and hand-torn
 into pieces
1 2 pound beef tenderloin,
 preferably center-cut
2 to 4 tablespoons canola oil
Kosher salt and freshly ground
 black pepper
Sautéed Pluots and Red Wine
 Reduction (*recipe follows*)
Potatoes Anna (*recipe follows*)

Ancho- and Pepita-Crusted Beef Medallions

Prepare the Sautéed Pluots and Red-Wine Reduction and the Potatoes Anna.

Put the pepitas in a spice mill or clean coffee grinder and buzz until the seeds become a coarse powder. Transfer the ground pepitas to a mixing bowl. Put the ancho chiles in the spice mill and grind until they form a powder. Combine the ancho powder with the ground pumpkin seeds and mix to distribute evenly.

Preheat the oven to 375°F. Trim the fat from the beef tenderloin and set aside the scraps to use in the sauce. Using a sharp knife, cut the beef into 4 equal medallions; season all sides with salt and pepper. Put a large skillet over medium-high heat and film with 2 tablespoons of oil. Working in batches so as not to overcrowd the pan, sear both sides until brown, about 2 to 3 minutes each, adding more oil if needed. Once seared, roll the medallions in the ancho-pepitas mixture while they are still hot; the moisture will help bind the mix to the meat to form a crust. Transfer to a sheet pan and bake the beef medallions in the oven for 10 minutes.

Place a medallion in the center of each plate. Surround with the sautéed pluots. Drizzle the red-wine sauce all around and serve with the potatoes Anna.

> **Tip** Salt meats well in advance of cooking to give the salt a chance to melt and penetrate the meat. (Chickens and roasts should be salted a day before cooking.) Contrary to conventional wisdom, salting meat does not dry it out. *Michael Ruhlman*

Sautéed Pluots and Red-Wine Reduction

Reserved beef scraps from the tenderloin
6 pluots or young plums, pitted and quartered
2 cups dry red wine, such as Pinot Noir
2 tablespoons honey
Kosher salt and freshly ground black pepper
2 tablespoons unsalted butter

Place a small saucepan over medium heat and add the beef scraps. Cook until the fat is rendered. Add 1 of the quartered pluots and sauté for 1 or 2 minutes to soften. Pour in the red wine and cook for 15 minutes until the liquid is thick enough to coat the back of a spoon. Strain the sauce into another pot, stir in the honey, and season with salt and pepper. Gently simmer over medium-low heat.

Heat a skillet over medium heat and add the butter. When the butter is foamy, toss in the remaining plum pieces and sauté until soft.

Potatoes Anna

3 large Idaho potatoes
¼ cup melted unsalted butter
Kosher salt and freshly ground black pepper

Preheat the oven to 375°F. Peel and rinse the potatoes. In a food processor fitted with a slicing blade, or with a mandoline or very sharp knife, slice the potatoes thinly; work quickly to prevent discoloration.

Brush the bottom of a 9-inch cast-iron skillet or round cake pan with about 1 tablespoon of the melted butter. Cover with a layer of potato slices, arranged in overlapping concentric circles. Brush the potatoes with melted butter and season with salt and pepper. Add 2 more layers of potatoes, brushing each layer with butter and seasoning with salt and pepper. Cover the pan with foil. Bake for 30 minutes, until the potatoes are tender. Remove the foil and continue to cook, uncovered, for 15 or 20 minutes until the potatoes are slightly browned on top.

To serve, place a large round platter upside-down over the skillet. Carefully flip the skillet and platter, inverting the potatoes Anna onto the platter.

Monte Cristo Cubano
with Maple Jus and Yellow Mustard *serves 4*

Chef Katie Hagan-Whelchel

1 tablespoon paprika
1 tablespoon ground coriander
1 teaspoon cumin
1½ teaspoons cayenne
¼ cup all-purpose flour
Finely grated zest of 2 limes
1 tablespoon oregano,
    preferably Mexican
2 tablespoons unsalted butter
4 smashed garlic cloves
4 fresh thyme sprigs
1 medium white onion,
    coarsely chopped
1 celery stalk, coarsely chopped
1 carrot, coarsely chopped
Kosher salt and freshly ground
    black pepper
2 tablespoons extra-virgin
    olive oil
3 pounds pork shoulder,
    trimmed of excess fat
    and cut in large cubes
2 tomatoes, coarsely chopped
1 quart chicken stock
1 bay leaf
1 teaspoon whole black
    peppercorns

Carnitas

Toast the paprika, coriander, cumin, and cayenne in a dry skillet over low heat for approximately 2 minutes until fragrant, shaking the pan to prevent scorching. Remove from heat and cool slightly. In a shallow bowl, mix the toasted spices with the flour, lime zest, and oregano. Set aside.

Place a large stockpot over medium-high heat and add the butter. When the butter foams, add the garlic, thyme, and onion; sauté for 1 minute until translucent. Add the celery and carrot; season with salt and pepper. Cook and stir the mirepoix (mixture) for at least 2 minutes to soften. Dump the mixture into a bowl and set aside.

Return the stockpot to the heat and film with the olive oil. Dredge the pork cubes in the seasoned flour mixture, making sure to coat all sides, and dust off any excess. Lay the pork cubes in the hot oil and brown on all sides, turning with tongs. Reduce the heat to medium-low and add the reserved mirepoix mixture, tomatoes, bay leaf, and peppercorns. Pour in the chicken stock and simmer, covered, for 45 minutes or until the pork is fork-tender. Meanwhile start the tempura batter.

½ cup cornstarch
¼ teaspoon salt
12 large egg whites
2 tablespoons cold water
Canola oil, for frying

Batter

Sift the cornstarch and salt, making sure there are no lumps. Put the egg whites in a bowl set in a bowl of ice. Whisk the whites until they are fluffy. Gradually add the cornstarch and salt. Continue to mix until the batter acquires a paste-like consistency. Whisk in the water. Keep the batter on ice so it stays fluffy. Refrigerate until ready to use.

4 individual Cuban
    or French rolls
2 large dill pickles, sliced
    lengthwise
½ pound sliced Swiss cheese
½ pound smoked ham, sliced
    paper-thin
2 tablespoons unsalted butter,
    at room temperature
½ cup yellow mustard
½ cup maple syrup mixed
    with 2 tablespoons water

Sandwiches

Heat about 3 inches of oil in a large heavy pot or deep fryer to 375°F. While the oil is heating, assemble the sandwiches.

Cut the rolls in half lengthwise, leaving the halves attached like a hinge. Layer one-quarter of the pickles on the top side of each roll, followed by one-quarter of the cheese. Distribute the smoked ham and carnitas among the bottom halves of the rolls. Press the two halves of the sandwiches together. Butter both sides of the sandwiches.

Place each sandwich in a preheated panini press and grill until the bread is toasted and the cheese begins to melt, about 2 minutes. Alternatively, place a griddle or nonstick pan over low heat, add the sandwiches and weigh them down with a can or heavy pot to flatten. (Use a brick wrapped in foil if nothing else is available.) Cook for 3 minutes on each side until the cheese is melted and the bread is toasted and slightly crisp; make sure the bread does not burn.

Secure each sandwich with a couple of toothpicks positioned vertically to hold it together. Dip the entire sandwich in the batter to coat evenly. Gently lower the sandwich into the hot oil and deep-fry until golden brown, about 2 minutes. Carefully remove the sandwiches and place on a platter lined with paper towels. Slice the sandwiches in half diagonally and serve with yellow mustard and maple jus on the side for dipping.

Pulled-Pork Pasta with Almond Cream Sauce *serves 4*

Chef Sara Lawson

4 crushed garlic cloves

3 tablespoons dark-brown sugar

3 tablespoons soy sauce

3 tablespoons hot sauce,
  such as Sriracha

¼ cup canola oil

1 pound boneless pork butt,
  cut into large cubes

Kosher salt and freshly ground
  black pepper

1 cup dry white wine, such as
  Sauvignon Blanc

1 carrot, large dice

1 leek, white part only, washed
  and chopped

1 chopped onion

3 bay leaves

½ teaspoon whole black
  peppercorns

1 tablespoon fennel seed

1 pound fresh or dried
  pappardelle or other long
  flat pasta

Almond Cream Sauce
  (recipe on page 62)

Fresh flat-leaf parsley, for garnish

Pulled-Pork Pasta

Combine the garlic, brown sugar, soy sauce, hot sauce, and oil in a mixing bowl and stir to combine. Add the pork cubes, tossing to coat. Cover and marinate for 30 minutes or up to overnight in the refrigerator.

Preheat the oven to 325°F. Place a large Dutch oven or heavy-bottomed pot over medium-high heat. Put the pork and marinade in the hot pan. Sear the cubes evenly on all sides until browned, turning with tongs. While browning, season the meat in stages with salt and pepper. Just before the garlic burns, deglaze with the wine, scraping up the brown bits on the bottom of the pot with a wooden spoon. Cook until the wine is almost totally evaporated, about 3 minutes. Add the carrot, leek, onion, bay leaves, peppercorns, and fennel seed. Pour in enough cold water to cover by 1 inch. Cover the pot and braise in the oven for 1½ to 2 hours until the pork is fork-tender.

Pour 1 cup of the braising liquid into a saucepan and simmer over medium heat until reduced by half; taste for seasoning. Leave the pork in the remaining liquid so it stays moist. When the meat is cool enough to handle, shred it with your fingers. Return to the liquid and keep warm and covered.

Bring a large pot of salted water to the boil. Add the pasta ribbons to the boiling water and cook until *al dente*, 8 to 10 minutes. Drain the pasta, put it in a bowl, and toss lightly with ½ cup of the almond cream sauce.

To serve, divide the pasta among 4 plates. Top with the shredded pork, a drizzle of the reduced braising liquid, and more almond cream sauce. Garnish with parsley.

2 cups whole almonds,
 lightly toasted
1 quart heavy cream
Kosher salt and freshly ground
 black pepper

Almond Cream Sauce

Combine the almonds and cream in a saucepan and place over medium heat. Slowly simmer for 30 minutes, stirring often. Strain out the almonds and discard. Continue to simmer until the cream coats the back of a spoon, about 30 minutes. Season to taste and hold hot.

> **Tip** Adding a bit of pasta water to your pasta sauce will give it extra body. *Todd English*

Shrimp 'n Grits *serves 4*

Chef Katie Hagan-Whelchel

2 cups chopped smoked bacon

1 tablespoon extra-virgin olive oil

1 yellow onion, medium dice

5 minced garlic cloves

1 carrot, medium dice

1 celery stalk, medium dice

2 tomatoes, seeded and chopped

3 fresh thyme sprigs

Kosher salt and freshly ground
    black pepper

1 tablespoon plus 1 teaspoon
    cayenne

½ cup dry white wine, such as
    Sauvignon Blanc

Juice of 1 lemon

5 cups chicken stock

¼ cup (½ stick) unsalted butter

1 cup yellow polenta or
    stone-ground cornmeal

4 ounces cream cheese,
    at room temperature

16 large shrimp (about
    1½ pounds)

2 tablespoons chopped fresh
    chives, plus more for garnish

Preheat the oven to 400°F. In a large sauté pan over medium heat, fry the bacon until it begins to brown and turn crispy. Pull the pan off the heat and transfer the bacon bits to a plate lined with paper towels. Strain the rendered bacon grease and keep it handy.

Heat a large oven-proof skillet over medium-high flame. Coat with the olive oil and 2 tablespoons of the bacon fat. When the oil is hot, add the onion, garlic, carrot, celery, tomatoes, and thyme; season with salt, pepper, and 1 tablespoon of cayenne. Sauté for 2 minutes until the vegetables begin to soften. Deglaze with the white wine and lemon juice. Pour in 1 cup of the stock and stir to combine. Place the entire pan in the oven and roast for 25 minutes.

Meanwhile, place a 3-quart pot over medium-high heat. Add the butter and the remaining 4 cups of chicken stock and bring to a boil. Slowly whisk in the cornmeal, stirring constantly. When the grits begin to bubble, turn the heat to medium-low and simmer for 8 to 10 minutes, stirring constantly. Season with salt and pepper. Add the cream cheese and stir until the grits are smooth and thick. Set aside on low heat to keep warm.

The vegetable mixture should be slightly charred by now. Use a handheld or conventional blender to purée the roasted vegetables into a thick sauce. Taste and adjust seasoning if needed. Cover to keep warm.

Season the shrimp well with salt, pepper, and the remaining teaspoon of cayenne. Heat 2 tablespoons of the reserved bacon fat in a large sauté pan. When it is hot, lay the shrimp in the pan to cover the bottom. Season again with salt and pepper. Sauté until the shrimp turn pink and curl up. Toss in the chives and stir for about 20 seconds to combine. Do not overcook.

To serve, mound the grits on 4 plates. Lay 4 shrimp on top of each mound and spoon the sauce all around. Garnish with the reserved bacon bits and a sprinkle of chives.

Crème Fraîche and Honey Egg Custard with French Meringue *serves 4*

Chef Katsuji Tanabe

"This is the most simple egg dish that I have ever cooked and it represents my way of life" says chef Tanabe. "Don't follow everybody else."

4 large eggs
¼ cup honey
½ cup crème fraîche
3 tablespoons milk
1 vanilla bean, split lengthwise
    and scraped
½ cup powdered sugar
1 teaspoon ground cinnamon

Carefully crack off the top third of the eggs, using a knife. Keep the shells intact for serving. Separate the whites and yolks.

To make the custard, bring a pot of water to a simmer over medium-low heat. Combine the egg yolks, honey, crème fraîche, milk, and vanilla in a metal or glass heat-resistant bowl and whisk until smooth. Set the bowl over the simmering water, without letting the bottom touch the water, and continue to whisk until the custard is very thick and yellow. Don't let it boil. Remove the bowl from the heat. Using a small spoon, fill the reserved eggshells with the custard and chill in the refrigerator.

Put the egg whites in the bowl of an electric mixer fitted with a wire-whisk attachment. Whip on high speed until the egg whites are fluffy and hold soft peaks, about 3 minutes. With the mixer running, rain the powdered sugar into the whites until the meringue becomes glossy and holds stiff peaks.

To serve, nest each egg custard cup on a small plate surrounded by a cloth napkin to hold it steady (This can be tricky.) Put a dollop of meringue on each and dust lightly with cinnamon.

COOKING UNDER FIRE

43-Minute Mango Mousse Ice Cream with Tempura-Battered Berries *serves 4*

Chef Katsuji Tanabe

"This recipe is just to show off my culinary knowledge in being able to present ice cream on the table in less than an hour," says chef Tanabe.

4 ripe mangos, halved, pitted, peeled, and coarsely chopped
½ cup sugar
2 cups heavy whipping cream
1 box of kosher salt
Lots of ice
1 pint pomegranate juice
Tempura-Battered Berries
    (recipe follows)

Mango Mousse Ice Cream

Puree the mango and sugar in a blender or food processor until completely smooth. In a chilled bowl, whip the heavy cream until it holds soft peaks. Gently fold the mango puree into the whipped cream a bit at a time. Transfer the mango mousse to a small metal bowl or pot.

Put the ice and salt in a large round pot or other metal container. Nestle the pot of mango mousse in the ice mixture and whisk vigorously to incorporate air. Put the whole thing in the freezer for 5 minutes. Remove from the freezer and whisk to aerate the mixture and break up parts that begin to freeze. Return to the freezer for 5 minutes. Repeat this process 5 times until the ice cream is fluffy and begins to harden, about 30 minutes. Keep the ice cream in the freezer while preparing the rest of the dish.

Cook the pomegranate juice in a small pot over medium heat until it becomes a syrup, thick enough to coat the back of a spoon. Remove from heat and cool to room temperature.

To serve, scoop the mango mousse ice cream into 4 martini glasses or shallow dessert bowls. Drizzle the pomegranate syrup on top and garnish with 3 or 4 Tempura-Battered Berries.

(continued)

Peanut or canola oil,
   for deep-frying
¼ cup rice flour
¼ cup all-purpose flour
2 tablespoons cornstarch,
   plus more for dusting
Ice-cold water or seltzer,
   as needed (about ¾ cup)
½ cup fresh blueberries
   or raspberries

Tempura-Battered Berries

Prepare the battered berries immediately before serving.

Heat about 1 inch of oil in a large heavy pot or deep fryer to 375°F. While the oil is heating, mix the flours and cornstarch in a large bowl. Whisk in the ice water until the consistency resembles pancake batter and there are no lumps.

Spread about ¼ cup of cornstarch on a shallow plate. Roll the berries in the cornstarch, shaking off the excess. Dip the berries into the batter one by one to coat lightly but completely, letting the excess drip back into the bowl. Gently lower the tempura-battered berries into the hot oil. Fry for 5 seconds until the coating is light golden and crisp. Remove carefully with a slotted spoon and drain on a plate lined with paper towels.

COOKING
UNDER FIRE

Thyme-Infused Crème Brûlée *serves 4*

Chef Katie Hagan-Whelchel

2 cups heavy cream
6 sprigs fresh thyme
4 large egg yolks
½ cup sugar, plus extra
    for dusting

Pour the cream into a pot and place over medium-low heat. Bring to a simmer briefly; do not boil or it will overflow. Remove from the heat and add the thyme; let it steep in the cream for several minutes. Remove the thyme and discard.

Preheat the oven to 325°F. In a large bowl, whisk the egg yolks and sugar until the mixture is thick and pale yellow, about 3 minutes. Gradually whisk the hot cream into the yolk-and-sugar mixture. (Do not add the hot cream too quickly or the eggs will cook.)

Divide the custard into four 6-ounce ramekins or brûlée molds, filling three-quarters full. Arrange the ramekins in a shallow baking pan. Pour hot tap water into the baking dish until it reaches halfway up the sides of the ramekins; be careful not to get any water in the custard. Bake until custard is barely set around the edges, about 35 minutes; the centers should jiggle slightly. Remove from the oven and let the ramekins cool in the water bath for about 10 minutes. Then put them in the refrigerator to chill for at least 1 hour.

Sprinkle 1 tablespoon of sugar on top of each chilled custard. Hold a kitchen torch 2 inches above the surface to brown the sugar and form a crust. If you do not have a torch, use a broiler but keep a close eye on it. Serve at once.

Master Pantry

The finalists were provided these basic ingredients with which to work:

- Kosher salt

- Sea Salt

- Peppercorns: black, white, pink, green, and Szechwan

- Dry spices: cayenne, cumin seeds, fennel seeds, coriander seeds, curry powder, paprika, cardamom, turmeric, wasabi powder, etc.

- Oils: olive, canola, grapeseed, and sesame

- Vinegars: rice, champagne, and balsamic

- Red and white wine

- Sake

- Soy sauce

- Dijon mustard

- Chicken stock

- Flours: all-purpose, rice flour, and cornmeal

- Cornstarch

- Sugar

- Honey

- Milk

- Heavy cream

- Sour cream

- Yogurt

- Butter

- Eggs

- Mirepoix ingredients: onions, garlic, celery, carrots

- Fresh herbs: thyme, bay leaves, rosemary, chervil, chives, flat-leaf parsley, basil, etc.

Tip To toast spices: place spices in a dry pan over medium heat. Shake frequently to prevent burning. Cook for 2 minutes or until fragrant.

Who's Who: Finalists' Biographies

John Paul Abernathy

A native of southern California, J.P. discovered a love of cuisine in Napa Valley, inspired by its rich landscape and myriad culinary influences. His interest in cooking led to stints in France and Switzerland and finally at the Culinary Institute of America.

William Barlow

This Mississippi native learned respect for raw ingredients as a child, handpicking vegetables from his grandfather's garden and shrimping with his dad. But it wasn't until years later, during a trip to Boston, that a taste of cassoulet evoked an epiphany about his future. To his parents' dismay, he left a dot-com job to become a cook at a local eatery and then headed to Boston with fifty dollars in his pocket. Work at respected Boston restaurants offered lessons in the art and style of the culinary world and the business of running a restaurant, knowledge he puts to use as a lead cook and butcher in New Orleans.

Michael Duronslet

Raised near New Orlean's famous French Quarter, Michael grew up with family values that included lessons in love from the kitchen. Before he could reach the stove, his parents would pull up a chair so he could stir the roux. Since then, Michael's culinary career has been propelled by some encounters with fate—and with his wife! For Michael, the opportunity to make a living as a chef is the equivalent of being a superstar athlete. Michael draws inspiration from those around him: his wife is from Trinidad, his parents Creole, his bosses Middle Eastern.

Katie Hagen Whelchel

This self-described "classy redneck" was born and raised in Kentucky. Katie developed a love for food at an early age based on a simple philosophy: survival of the fittest. After learning to piece together simple meals, she began to enjoy cooking; her passion was guided by her brother, also a chef. For Katie, cooking involves constant learning, and perpetual efforts to figure out new approaches and methods.

Blair King

Born in the Missouri Ozarks, Blair calls the kitchen "a home away from home." His passion for food began when he was a thirteen-year-old washing dishes and making pizzas. In L.A. after high school, Blair was introduced to a whole new world of flavors, spices, and cultures. While attending art school in Seattle, Blair says, it hit him like a thrown fish at Pike Place Market: he was an artist, alright, but his medium was food. Now, he says, each day at his job as a sous chef is a thrill and a challenge, and cooking for guests and celebrities at his restaurant's exposition counter is a dream come true.

Sara Lawson

A native of Southern California, Sara was encouraged very early to indulge in the pleasures of the natural world. Her natural love of entertaining drew her attention to the ways people interact with food, from preparing it to consuming it. A graduate of the California Culinary Academy, Sara plans to open her own restaurant one day. She has decided that her purpose in life is to learn, teach, laugh, and eat.

Matthew Leeper

This former Army Ranger, born on an U.S. Air Force base in the Philippines, believes that he didn't find his calling as a chef—it found him. Traveling the world with his military family, Matt acquired an extensive knowledge of food. His zeal grew as he progressed from a first job as a busser and oyster shucker to work in the Ranger dining facility after injuries kept him from the front lines. Encouraged by a fellow Army chef, Matt went on to pursue his passion in culinary school.

Autumn Maddox

Autumn spent her early childhood on a modest farm in Washington state that introduced her to garden-fresh foods along with the world of chickens, pigs, and horses. This foundation gave rise to a passion for the bounty of the sea, fresh organic produce, and locally raised meat, poultry, and eggs that continues to drive her career. Deeply aware that food delivers much more than nourishment, Autumn is rewarded by the looks of contentment, surprise, and delight on people's faces when they taste her culinary creations.

Yannick Marchand

A native of France, Yannick discovered his love of food at a very early age in his grandmother's kitchen. She continues to inspire him, and her skill and gentleness inform his approach to cooking today. An avid cook since arriving in America over 15 years ago, Yannick is a graduate of the New England Culinary Institute. A resident of California, Yannick emphasizes the fresh, natural ingredients that first inspired him.

Jennifer L. McDermott

The youngest of four children, born and brought up in Illinois, Jennifer was partially raised by her great-grandparents. Helping them with recipes from their Mexican and Nicaraguan heritages, she became enthralled with cooking and discovered a talent for improvisation. Jennifer still watches old videos of her great-grandparents cooking. She understands the importance of hard work in a culinary career, and loves that cooking will always be a learning experience.

Russell Moore

His hometown, Chicago, may be known for its deep-dish pizza, but Russell's passion in the kitchen is the lively tastes of Cajun and Caribbean cuisine. Russell's first cooking project, at age seven, was popping popcorn and "making enough for a small nation." A culinary-school graduate with experience as a chef in hotels, nightclubs, a racetrack, and a senior-citizen home, Russell is now a freelance restaurant consultant and vice president of a company known for its "homicide salsa."

Katsuji Tanabe

The son of a Japanese mechanical engineer and a Mexican dentist, Katsuji grew up with the expectation that he would follow his father into engineering. But his love for cooking prompted him to volunteer to work as a dishwasher just to spend time in a professional kitchen. During his teen years, his parents divorced and everything changed: he began working as a cook to make ends meet. Katsuji eventually moved to Los Angeles, where he received his culinary degree from a community college and continued to work in kitchens throughout the city.

COOKING
UNDER FIRE

Acknowledgments

This companion book to PBS's series *Cooking Under Fire* has been made possible by the creative talents of many people who went above and beyond on the television series. For the book, we especially thank the following individuals: JoAnn Cianciulli, food editor and writer extraordinaire, who also worked as the culinary producer on the series; Alison Kennedy, series designer, and Tyler Kemp-Benedict, both of whom designed this book; Stephanie Coyle, Betsy Groban, Julie Gomes, Jennifer Welsh, Lenore Lanier Gibson, Lisa Abitbol, Hilary Finkel Buxton, and Blyth Lord, for coordinating this effort; Ann Goodsell, copy editor; and all the chefs, from our celebrity judges and guest chefs to the finalists themselves, whose vision and culinary excellence are what it's all about!

And to our sponsors, who believed in and supported the concept and helped bring it to public television, we say a special thanks: Chrysler, Contessa Premium Foods Inc., All-Clad Metalcrafters LLC, WGBH Educational Foundation, and public television viewers.

THANK YOU!

W Lance Reynolds
John Rieber
Laurie Donnelly

Finalist John Paul Abernathy prepares his dish.